W9-ASI-214

THE WALLS ARE TALKING

ABBY JOHNSON

With Kristin Detrow

THE WALLS
ARE
TALKING

Former
Abortion Clinic Workers
Tell Their Stories

IGNATIUS PRESS   SAN FRANCISCO

Cover art © Shutterstock

Cover design by Roxanne Mei Lum

© 2016 by Ignatius Press, San Francisco
All rights reserved
ISBN 978-1-62164-250-3
Library of Congress Control Number 2014959913
Printed in the United States of America ∞

This book is dedicated to the men and women who have allowed me to be a part of their journey out of the abortion industry. Your courage inspires me every day. You are the definition of bravery. You will never know how honored I am to be a small part of your lives.

CONTENTS

PREFACE

This will not be an enjoyable read. It is a necessary one, however, as it narrates the real-life experiences of former abortion clinic workers who agreed to be interviewed for this book, as well as some of my own. To protect their privacy and mine, I have written all the stories in the first person so that you, the reader, will not be able to distinguish one voice from another. As you read these harrowing accounts, please keep the real people who had these experiences in your prayers. These courageous individuals, who have left their jobs in the abortion industry, have come forward with their stories, not for fame or notoriety, but to make a difference. They want their stories to change the lives of others for the better. They want their past mess to become a message.

ABBY'S INTRODUCTION

If These Walls Could Talk

"There's one question only a woman can answer," declares the tagline of HBO's *If These Walls Could Talk.* The cover boasts a stunning trio of veteran actresses along with Siskel and Ebert's highly coveted "Two thumbs up!"

Of course, moviegoers would expect nothing less from a film starring the likes of Demi Moore, Sissy Spacek, and Cher. The 1996 film amazed the network by becoming HBO's highest-rated made-for-TV movie to date. Much more than mere entertainment, *If These Walls Could Talk* provoked the minds of Generation Xers to ponder the highly divisive issue of abortion.

If These Walls Could Talk proudly bills itself as "a powerful, intimate portrait of how times and freedoms have changed. It will shock you. It will surprise you. And no matter where you stand on the issue, it will force you to think again."

Although critics and fans wholeheartedly agree that the film is powerful and does indeed paint an intimate portrait, the brushstroke's finished work is nothing less than propaganda at its finest.

Using three vignettes spaced twenty-two years apart and set in the backdrop of the same house, *If These Walls Could*

Talk chronicles three women who are faced with unintentional pregnancy and how access to abortion was restricted or hindered by legal constraints and societal views in each decade.

Claire (Demi Moore) is a grief-stricken young widow living in a Chicago suburb in 1952. She becomes pregnant after a drunken tryst with her brother-in-law. Anxious to avoid humiliation and further heartache for her dead husband's family, Claire desperately seeks an illegal abortion. Along the way she is met with cold-hearted judgment and skittish sympathizers. Claire's procedure is finally performed by a sketchy travelling abortionist on her kitchen table. The illegal abortion causes her to hemorrhage and ultimately to die.

The second segment features Barbara (Sissy Spacek), a frazzled policeman's wife and mother of four. Barbara's hopes and dreams have been placed on the back burner for years, and she is practically a slave to her husband and children. Finally taking the time to focus on herself, Barbara returns to college and seems to have her feet set firmly on the path to fulfillment until an accidental pregnancy tosses a monkey wrench into her plans. Although encouraged by both a post-abortive friend and self-actualized daughter to exercise her recently legalized right to choose abortion, in the end she isn't strong enough to make the decision. Ever a martyr to her family, Barbara sullenly continues the pregnancy.

Fast-forward to 1996. The house is now occupied by Christine (Anne Heche), a promising college student who finds herself impregnated by her married professor. Christine's decision to abort is not made flippantly. She rejects the idea on her first visit to the clinic. Despite the pleas of her Jesus-loving best friend and the drone-like protestors at the clinic, Christine returns intent on going through with the abortion. The procedure goes smoothly until a pro-life terrorist bursts through the door, mortally shooting the heroic abortionist (Cher).

The delicate subtlety this movie employs is both genius and insidiously effective. Young viewers who haven't been taught to think critically or spent much time considering the complex issue of abortion scarcely stand a chance against the highly sympathetic characters portrayed in *If These Walls Could Talk*. The unwanted pregnancies seem impossible and abortion the only sensible answer.

Unwittingly, the audience finds itself hopeful that some brave doctor will perform an illegal procedure, rescuing Claire from her risky self-abortion attempts; silently urging Barbara, finally choosing to invest in herself, to terminate her pregnancy; disgusted by the tactless and judgmental pro-life crazies; and horror-struck when one of them violently takes the life of the self-sacrificing abortionist.

Aldous Huxley said, "The propagandist's purpose is to make one set of people forget that the other set of people are human." *If These Walls Could Talk* undoubtedly succeeds in completely glossing over the fact that for every woman daunted by an unwanted pregnancy, there is another life at stake: an innocent human—a life easily marginalized and depicted solely as a burden; a quandary; an affliction from which hapless women can only be rescued by safe and legal abortion.

The abortion clinic I directed in Bryan, Texas, had a room where women sat and waited for their procedures. There was a door that connected this room to the clinic's common areas. Staff members were instructed that those doors must remain locked at all times. For me, it was a hassle to stop and rifle through my keys when moving about the clinic.

But really, it bothered me for an entirely different reason. Something about having those women locked in that room just seemed wrong to me. As if they were trapped there. Finally, I confronted my supervisor about it. She responded by insisting that I watch *If These Walls Could Talk*. Young and gullible, I completely bought into the lies and was sucked in by the masterful propaganda. One viewing was all it took to convince me fully that a locked door was a minor inconvenience we must suffer to ensure the safety of the clinic staff and our patients.

* * * * *

Multiple volumes could be penned expounding on the flawed logic and distortions in the three scenarios presented in *If These Walls Could Talk*. While it is vital to meet these lies with truth, that is not the goal of this project. Randy Alcorn did a fabulous job of answering difficult questions in his book *ProLife Answers to Pro-Choice Questions*.[1]

The Bible teaches that our testimony is a powerful tool for defeating evil. Revelation 12:11 says, "They have conquered him by the blood of the Lamb and by the word of their testimony." Sharing my own story of being a post-abortive mother and former Planned Parenthood clinic director has become my life's work.

September 26, 2009, was like any other normal work day at the clinic until I was unexpectedly asked to assist

[1] Randy Alcorn, *ProLife Answers to ProChoice Questions*, expanded and updated, rev. ed. (Sisters, Ore.: Multnomah Publishers, 2000).

with an ultrasound-guided abortion. I was excited about the prospect. After all, I was Planned Parenthood's 2008 Employee of the Year. My personal ambition was to become Planned Parenthood's chief operating officer, and I was on the fast track to meeting that goal. Having never seen an ultrasound-guided abortion, I relished another opportunity to gain knowledge and understanding.

Instead of receiving training that would advance my Planned Parenthood career, what I witnessed on that screen instantaneously opened my eyes to the terror of abortion. I was no longer able to suppress the truth about my career—nor justify my own abortions. As I stood watching, a thirteen-week-old unborn child struggled and ultimately lost its life within its mother's womb, finally crumpling and disappearing into the cannula, a hollow plastic tube attached to the suction machine by a flexible hose.

* * * * *

To this day I continually grapple with guilt, shame, and the heaviness of regret. I am passionate about sharing my story and doggedly determined to educate people about the reality of abortion. I want them to know the truth about what it does to men, women, and babies. That is the very heart and soul of this book.

In 1996, *If These Walls Could Talk* persuaded a generation that abortion was necessary and that those who oppose it are either ignorant freaks or violent religious zealots. *The Walls Are Talking* is a compilation of stories, some my own plus those of others whose lives have been forever altered by abortion. Although it will be difficult to read, and at times tough to fathom, the clinic walls will speak through these women, and it will be a beautiful thing as the light of truth and forgiveness illuminates a dark place.

My fervent prayer is that by being transparent and sharing their experiences, these brave women will find healing and newness of life, and that their stories will expose abortion for what it is. I pray that babies will be saved, women will be deterred from making such a hopeless choice, and men will encourage and support their partners to choose life. If you have never been faced with a crisis pregnancy or worked in the abortion industry, I implore you to impart an extra measure of grace and compassion as you read.

As Jesus said in John 8:7, "Let him who is without sin among you be the first to throw a stone at her."

Three Hundred Forty-Seven Dollars

It was business as usual at our abortion clinic. Saturdays were typically our busiest day for abortions, and this one was certainly no exception. A woman in her early twenties arrived with a friend for her procedure.

Although I counseled this woman prior to her abortion, nothing about her particularly stood out in my memory. As scores of women had before her, she sat in my office and listened to my carefully worded and well-rehearsed Planned Parenthood–approved spiel. And as is the case with the majority of the women I counseled, she signed the mountain of obligatory paperwork without bothering to skim it—had she attempted to, it's doubtful that she would have comprehended a word. Then she returned to the waiting room, one step closer to ending the life of her ten-week-old baby.

I continued about my business, and like the countless women I encountered at the clinic on a daily basis, she didn't cross my mind again—that is, until Wednesday, when we received a call from her informing us that she had been admitted to the hospital. She claimed that we had "left some of the baby". She had to endure a D&C to remove the leftover fetal parts and was being treated with IV antibiotics for a serious infection.

Of course, we didn't believe her. Although abortion advocates are constantly spouting slogans declaring their unwavering love and devotion to women, in reality, it is commonplace for some clinic workers to ignore, marginalize, blame, and ridicule the women who trust them—especially those who become confrontational when dissatisfied with services rendered by the clinic.

Don't misunderstand. We didn't start our careers jaded. Like me, the majority of my fellow workers were drawn to the abortion industry out of an authentic desire to serve women and families in crisis. However, after working day in and day out for an organization that charges large sums of money to end the lives of unborn babies, no matter what philosophical spin you put on it, inevitably, our once tender hearts grew the necessary calluses. As a result, the confused and vulnerable women that sought solace at the clinic were oftentimes met with icy professionalism and indifference.

To verify the woman's story, we were able to obtain her medical records through HIPAA's Continuation of Care. The pathology lab report from the D&C indicated that indeed there had been "fetal parts" left in her uterus.

As the clinic director, I knew this was a massive problem. We had failed this client in at least two major ways. First, the doctor had not performed a complete abortion. Secondly, the POC (Products of Conception) technician, who just happened to be my supervisor at the time, had blatantly botched her job.

Each clinic that performs abortions has a POC tech charged with the grisly duty of reassembling the aborted baby to ensure that no parts are left inside the patient. A quick check of the client's paperwork confirmed that the abortionist and my supervisor had signed off, stating that all of the fetal parts were present and accounted for.

In this particular case, the facts simply could not be denied. The client had come to us for a service, one that our rehearsed talking points insisted is safe, effective, and very unlikely to carry any long-term side effects. Yet, there she was in the hospital. The mere thought of her made me squirm.

I could picture her in the hospital bed, receiving intravenous antibiotics to fight off a life-threatening infection and undergoing yet another painful procedure to remove the remnants of the fetus she had trusted us to do away with. Deep inside my core, an indictment was released and bubbled to the surface. *You have bought into a lie. You are not helping women.* As I had numerous times, I pushed my doubts away and focused on extinguishing the fire that was presently burning in my lap. She was threatening to go to the media.

Menacing callers threatening to contact media outlets were hardly a rarity at the clinic. Even if there was some validity to the complaint of the client in question, as a staff we weren't usually unnerved by their threats. After all, most women would prefer not to parade in front of local news cameras complaining about the details of their abortions. It was documented medical evidence in this woman's case that caused the admin staff to fly into headless-chicken mode. Finally, my supervisor met with the Medical Services Committee, and they decided on a tried-and-true plan of action: hush money.

Several days later, the woman was released from the hospital. The clinic must have been one of her first stops. The Medical Services Committee had decided to grant her 897 dollars for her misfortune, but with one catch. In order to receive the money, she was required to sign a nondisclosure agreement stating that she would not then, nor ever, go public with her complications. She did so, again, without even bothering to skim the document.

The fee for her abortion was 550 dollars. This money was not returned to her.

Even then, completely sold out to the cause of reproductive rights, I wanted to shake the woman. I wanted to snatch the pen and prevent her from signing her rights away, to keep her from settling for such a paltry and insulting figure for all that she had endured at our hands.

But I didn't. Because I was wholeheartedly devoted to an industry that thrives on the premise that life is cheap. Three hundred and forty-seven dollars, to be exact.

2

Medication Abortion

French child prodigy, inventor, and Catholic philosopher Blaise Pascal once said, "Evil is easy, and has infinite forms." My twenty-something self was still far from convinced that abortion was evil. I was most definitely in the market for a fix of the quick and easy variety. For the second time, I found myself faced with an unintended and quite unwelcome pregnancy.

I was eight weeks along, and the father was my husband, whom I was in the process of divorcing. The years I had spent with him and the way I had seen him parent, or fail to parent, his existing children from a previous relationship was enough to convince me that I simply could not, would not, bear this man's child.

Considering that I was a clinic volunteer at the time, radically supported the cause, and had surrounded myself with abortion-minded people, I played no mental ping-pong regarding my decision to terminate the pregnancy. More time was spent deliberating my abortion options.

A few years prior I'd had a surgical abortion. Although I had no complications with that procedure, I'd heard much about medication abortion and I was intrigued. Something about it seemed holistic in nature, noninvasive, and private. There were no stirrups or speculums to

be endured. And the best part was that the entire process could take place within the confines of my very own
home, on my schedule and with my dignity fully intact.

If that wasn't progress in feminism, well, I certainly
didn't know what was. After effortlessly filling out some
paperwork and going for some basic lab tests and an ultrasound, I was tucked into a room for my obligatory pre-
abortion chat. I had brought a friend with me, but support
persons are never permitted past the waiting room and I
was forced to wait alone. My pre-abortion "counseling"
session is forever etched into my mind with the detail and
permanence of the presidents' heads on Mount Rushmore.

"You will have some heavy bleeding and period-like
cramps," the worker assured me. "None of it should last
too long, and you should be back to normal in a couple
of days."

"Sounds good," I remember saying.

And it did. A couple of pills, a heavy period, and in
only a few days' time I'd be as good as new. If there were
any risks or side effects to these miracle drugs, she had
never mentioned them with me. As a young and idealistic
abortion-advocate recruit, I fully trusted that they had my
best interest at heart. If there was pertinent information
about these drugs that I needed to know, they would have
fallen all over themselves to provide it. That was why we
existed, after all, to be of service to women in crisis.

With confidence, I traded my four hundred dollars in
cash for a mifepristone (Mifeprex) pill and a brown bag of
medication to take at home. As promised, I suffered no ill
side effects from the first pill; in fact, I felt great.

The next day I was an obedient patient who meticu-
lously followed orders. After eating a light lunch, I took

the medication from my brown bag, four pills called miso-prostol. I had been warned that these pills would start my bleeding and cramping probably within an hour, but that it wouldn't be intolerable and that an ibuprofen or two would easily manage the discomfort.

I fashioned a cozy nest for myself in my bed and flipped on the TV, intent on enduring this minor physical trial like a trooper. As I channel surfed, I attempted to disregard the emotional ramifications of what I was about to do—in fact, what I had already done by swallowing those tablets. In ten minutes' time, I didn't need the assistance of the television or remote control to distract me.

Suddenly, I was blindsided by a pain in my abdomen like nothing I had ever experienced before or since. Then came the blood in a proverbial tidal wave. Somehow, I managed to hobble to the bathroom; the agony com-pounded with every step. The rush of blood was terrifying and unrelenting. Even the sturdiest of pads was powerless to absorb the flow.

All I could do was sit on the toilet, convinced that I was bleeding out. Intense pain would rack my stomach, and then lessen a bit. But the bleeding was constant. My misery was multiplied when the nausea hit. There I was, profusely bleeding into the toilet while vomiting into my bathroom trashcan. In between the flushing and heaving, I wept. Sweat literally poured out of me. This type of sweating, medically referred to as diaphoresis, has nothing to do with temperature. It is a result of excruciating pain.

After several hours on the toilet, I forced myself to feel cautiously hopeful that I might survive after all. I was weak, drenched with sweat and blood, and desperately wanted to take a bath. I continued to long for respite from the relentless cramps, and I was optimistic that the warm water might help. If nothing else, it would wash away the stench of the last few hours. My hair was matted with sweat and vomit. My legs were covered with a mixture of sweat and vomit mingled with blood.

I tentatively tried my legs and thankfully they cooperated. Exhausted and spent, I crept into my tub. The cramps continued to come in waves, but the warm water did seem to have a dulling effect on them. Grateful, I closed my eyes and rested my head on the edge of the tub. *Please, God,* I silently prayed. *Please let it be over.* In my weakened and fatigued state, I mercifully drifted into a semiconsciousness for a few minutes.

A fresh round of cramps forced me back to reality. My eyes snapped open, and what I saw horrified me. I lay frozen for a few seconds, my brain refusing to accept what I saw. My bathwater had turned to blood. I was lying in a crime scene. The metallic scent hit my nostrils and brought a new wave of nausea.

I knew one thing for certain. I had to get out of that tub. I had to wash the blood off of me. The horrific sight brought a surge of adrenaline to my weary body as I stood. I trembled and shook, and suddenly the effects of the adrenaline left as soon as it had come, leaving me faint. Again, I broke out in a cold sweat. Sobbing, I clung to the shower walls, intent on remaining vertical. I was utterly terrified of being immersed again in the gory mess at my feet.

At that point, I felt something break loose within me, and there was a splash in the bloody water draining out of the tub. I steadied myself and bent down to determine what in the world had come out of me. It was a blood clot the size of a lemon. I stared in disbelief. Was this my baby?

I didn't want to look at it. I just wanted it to be gone. With a clot that size, there was no way it simply was going to swirl down the drain. Using both hands, I was able to trap the clot and move it to the toilet. The majority of the mess had since drained, and I stood in the shower for a few minutes. The cramps didn't seem quite as intense.

The thought that this nightmare was finally over had no more than crossed my mind when I was struck with another excruciating pain in my abdomen. Doubled over, I yanked the curtain, fumbled out of the shower, and sat back onto the toilet. I passed another lemon-sized clot. And another, and another.

It was around midnight. I had been in agony in my bathroom for the better part of twelve hours. Still, the bleeding was far too intense even to consider returning to my bed. The clots had stopped passing with such rapid succession, but they continued to come nonetheless.

Eventually, the bleeding became more manageable and the clots ceased. Still, I didn't feel safe leaving the bathroom. I spent the night curled up on the bathroom floor. The cold tile felt good on my sweat-drenched face and body. Though I had never experienced exhaustion on such a level, sleep stubbornly refused to come. As I lay there, it occurred to me that this was the way I was going to die. I wondered who would find me. I prayed that it wouldn't be my mother.

This couldn't be normal, I thought. *I must be having some bizarre and extremely rare reaction to either mifepristone or misoprostol.* After all, what I had experienced was a far cry from the "heavy bleeding and period-like cramps" that I was cautioned against. I decided that if I lived through the night, I would call the clinic first thing in the morning.

Surely, they would want to examine me right away—or to be on the safe side, insist that I rush to the nearest emergency room.

You can imagine my surprise when the nurse returned my call the next day. Anxiously, I poured out the gruesome details of my ordeal and awaited her instructions.

"That's not abnormal," she said, barely disguising her disinterest.

"Not abnormal?" I seethed. The clotting, the pain, the insane amount of bleeding—she could not be serious.

"Use a heating pad, soak in a warm tub, and take some ibuprofen."

It was a good thing for this woman that she was safely out of my grasp. I was fuming, and she was poking the cobra. More than anything, I felt betrayed. The organization that I had given so much of myself to had completely failed to protect me.

I now look back on the tonsillectomy I had in 2009. The risks, benefits, and possible complications of the procedure had been explained to me ad nauseam during my pre-op visit with the ENT. Although he confidently assured me that such complications were extremely rare, he rattled off the list of possibilities nonetheless: severing of vocal cords resulting in an inability to speak; tooth and tongue damage—even death. The contrast between this visit and my pre-abortion "counseling" session at the clinic was striking.

I remember thinking that my ENT expounding on all the potential risks was total overkill. However, after giving it some thought, I was grateful that I was aware. I was informed. I had the *choice* to back out. Had I awoken having lost my ability to speak or with teeth busted out,

I would have at least recognized in advance that it was a possibility.

Although the lion's share of my nightmare with my mifepristone/misoprostol abortion occurred that awful night, it was a full eight weeks until my symptoms finally abated—eight weeks of blood clots; eight weeks of excruciating cramps; eight weeks of nausea.

In the end, my vitriol was no longer aimed at the clinic who had provided me with the medication, but at myself. Self-reproach and guilt consumed me—guilt that although I had endured an extremely harrowing physical ordeal, the ugly truth of the matter was that I was relieved that I was no longer pregnant.

After my eight-week reprieve, I resumed my role as a clinic volunteer. I vowed to do everything within my power never to let another woman go through what I had. When I advanced from volunteer to full-time staff at the clinic, I made it my personal mission to dissuade women from choosing this "natural" abortion method. I shared my story with them. My hatred of medication abortion became a joke around the clinic.

"Don't let her see the MAB [medical abortion] patients," my coworkers would banter. "They'll all choose surgical abortions, and we'll end up being here all day."

I didn't care. I knew it wasn't good for women. I knew that there was nothing natural about it. I was deeply troubled that this was being pushed on our patients. Never one to shy away from sharing my opinion, particularly pertaining to topics that I felt passionately about, I voiced my objections at a management meeting.

"Why aren't we telling women the risks?" I wanted to know.

My supervisor's answer mortified me. "We don't want to scare them."

"Scare them," I retorted. "Aren't they going to be scared when they think they're dying from the crazy amount of blood they're losing?"

After all, isn't the abortion spin machine constantly going on about how they "trust women"? Women have died from medication abortion. Thousands of women, myself included, have suffered serious complications. If they truly trusted women, wouldn't they do everything in their power to provide them with all the facts needed to make the right choice? Didn't they think that women were intelligent enough to make decisions regarding their bodies if they were presented with all the facts? Where was the female empowerment that I'd heard so much about at abortion-advocate rallies?

My protests were unappreciated and fell on deaf ears. Incapable of changing the powers that be, I settled for doing my part to prevent the women I personally counseled against this abortion method.

I now understand that the abortion industry is not concerned that women will be "scared". They are the ones who are scared—scared that if women did get accurate information and were aware of the risks of the lethal options on their malevolent menu, they would walk right out the door; and terrified that they would consider choosing life for their children. Every woman who walks out of the clinic and chooses life for her child equates to lost revenue.

When it comes to abortion providers, it's all about the Benjamins. Cold, hard cash will always be their bottom line. Since its approval by the Food and Drug Administration in

September of 2000, clinics have encouraged an increasing number of women to choose mifepristone and misoprostol to terminate their pregnancies.

Is the abortion industry aware of the risks? Yes. Do they know that women are dying each year from medication abortions? Yes. So why would they continue to advocate for this unsafe concoction while withholding the facts from women during their bogus counseling sessions?

Blaise Pascal understood why: "Evil is easy, and has infinite forms." Abortion is evil, and from a clinic's standpoint, medication abortion is easy. It's far less labor-intensive and time-consuming than surgical abortions, and it's highly profitable. Unfortunately, the road is not an easy one for the desperate and vulnerable women who are duped, misled, and outright lied to concerning this toxic mix.

Even when the drugs do terminate a pregnancy without the nightmarish complications that I and numerous others have suffered, the end result is a child's death, a reality that haunts many women throughout their entire lives. Having myself opted for both a surgical and medication abortion in addition to assisting countless women to do the same, I can attest to the fact that living with that truth is anything but easy.

3

Severed Feet and a Seared Conscience

On February 18, 2010, the Federal Bureau of Investigation and detectives from the Philadelphia District Attorney's Office raided the Women's Medical Society located at 3801-05 Lancaster Avenue in Philadelphia, Pennsylvania. The clinic's owner, Kermit Gosnell, was under investigation for controlled drug violations. Although Gosnell was indeed guilty of running a "pill mill", the seasoned investigators knew the second they entered the clinic that the prescription drug charges would be the tip of the iceberg.

According to the scathing 281-page grand jury report, "The clinic reeked of animal urine, courtesy of the cats that were allowed to roam (and defecate) freely. Furniture and blankets were stained with blood. Instruments were not properly sterilized."[1]

As investigators soldiered on into the heart of the "clinic", the horror of their findings intensified exponentially. Bags, jars, and jugs containing aborted fetuses in varying stages of development were strewn throughout the building, including the employee refrigerator. The emergency exit was ominously padlocked shut. Even the most basic medical equipment including a blood pressure cuff,

[1] R. Seth Williams, district attorney, Report of the Grand Jury XXII, First Juridical District of Pennsylvania, MISC. NO 0009901-2008, January 14, 2011.

defibrillator, and EKG machine were in disrepair. Medical goods meant to be used once and disposed of were kept and used over and over. The most horrific and baffling discovery that earned Gosnell the title "the Jeffrey Dahmer of Abortionists" were the jars of severed baby feet that lined the walls.

Philadelphia District Attorney Seth Williams headed the case against Gosnell. "He induced labor, forced the live birth of viable babies in the sixth, seventh and eighth month of pregnancy and then killed those babies by cutting into the back of the neck with scissors and severing their spinal cord," Williams said.[2]

It is unlikely that the full extent of the ghastly crimes committed at the clinic since it opened in 1972 will ever be discovered. In the end, Gosnell was charged with eight counts of murder. Seven of those counts were babies born alive and killed, often as he joked, and one count was for a woman who died as the result of a lethal dose of Demerol. Although the grand jury reports that the killings were routine and standard procedure at the Women's Medical Society, they could not prosecute more cases because files were destroyed.

Despite dozens of complaints against Gosnell and the staff at the clinic, state health officials failed to follow up. The Women's Medical Society hadn't been inspected at all since 1993. Gosnell applied for acceptance into the National Abortion Federation (NAF) in November of 2009, only one day after the death of a patient due to a Demerol overdose.

[2] Kevin Hayes, "Dr. Kermit Gosnell, Philadelphia Abortion Doctor, Accused of Killing 7 Babies with Scissors", CBS News, January 19, 2011, http://www .cbsnews.com/news/dr-kermit-gosnell-philadelphia-abortion-doctor-accused -of-killing-7-babies-with-scissors/.

The NAF sent a representative to the clinic December 14–15, 2009. The grand jury reports that the NAF evaluator called the Women's Medical Society the worst abortion clinic she had ever inspected. She cited numerous illegal and unsafe practices in the clinic, including failure to comply with Pennsylvania's twenty-four-hour waiting period for abortion, strong sedatives given to patients by untrained staff without a medical license, and leaving women totally unmonitored, sometimes overnight, after their procedures.

Although Gosnell's NAF application was denied, the organization failed to report their findings. According to the grand jury report, the NAF inspector "just never told anyone in authority about all the horrible, dangerous things she had seen". Because of a total regulatory failure on the part of the Pennsylvania's Department of Health and the NAF, Gosnell was free to abuse women and murder babies for the better part of four decades without any questions asked. In fact, it was completely accidental that Gosnell's horrific crimes were finally exposed at all.

I do not share this story for its obvious shock value. The Planned Parenthood that I directed was nothing like Gosnell's deplorable "clinic". In fact, I took great pride in the cleanliness of our facility and the compassionate care that the patients received. Bloody furniture, unsterilized equipment, and cat excrement would never have been tolerated. However, I have come to understand that despite our best efforts to run a safe and tidy clinic, in the end, we provided the same grisly service that Gosnell had. We murdered babies for profit.

Sure, our clients were not left alone to bleed out, or to deliver their ill-fated babies alive into toilets before they were killed with scissors. Instead, we used a curette to dismember and remove them from the mother in pieces. We would never have slapped, restrained, or physically and verbally abused our patients as Gosnell has been accused of doing on multiple occasions. My clinic opted to use calm and reassuring words to sell abortions to our patients.

The longer I have been out of the abortion business, the more perspective I have gained about the things I witnessed and participated in. I've come to realize that the employees of any clinic that performs abortions have more in common with the Gosnells of the world than they care to admit. I believe that those who work in the abortion industry are affected by a phenomenon I can only describe as the dulling of the conscience.

Conscience can be defined as an intuition or judgment of the intellect that distinguishes right from wrong. In 1 Timothy 4:2, even Paul writes about those who have had their consciences seared, or more literally, cauterized, through continual and unrepentant sin. Even the most militant pro-abortion activist presented with the facts of the case would have to admit that Gosnell and his crew were seriously lacking in the morality department.

I contend that abortion industry workers must have their consciences dulled in order to continue in their work. For me, the phenomenon started during my first conversation with an abortion activist and recruiter at a college volunteer fair. I distinctly remember how my stomach tightened at the mention of the word "abortion". I recall the inner discomfort I felt during my conversation with her.

The internal conflict that I felt was partially because I knew in my heart of hearts that abortion was wrong, but also because, while I believed that, I had secretly aborted my own child. I managed to push that gnawing feeling away, to squelch it. For the next eight years, I continued to muffle my conscience until it was practically an inaudible whisper, easily drowned out by the busyness of my life and the chaos in my mind.

There were moments of painful clarity during my career at an abortion clinic, moments that forced me to stop, think, and then make the decision to persist down the road I was on. Each decision further desensitized me to the truth of what I was doing and added to the callus that was forming around my heart. I had only been at the clinic for a few weeks when the powers that be decided that I could be trusted with the alarm code. Relieved that the code, 2229, was easy enough to remember, I didn't think anything else of it until a fellow worker informed me that management had chosen that particular code for a specific reason. The numbers corresponded on the dial pad with the letters to spell the word "baby".

A short time later I was trained to work in the clinic's Products of Conception (POC) lab. In the lab was a freezer where aborted fetuses were housed until the biohazard truck arrived. I was taken aback when I learned that this freezer had a name: "the Nursery". This sick gallows humor was something that could only be understood by a clinic insider. From an abortionist joking about the fetus he had just hacked up in a dish looking like barbecue, to office workers snickering about sending baby-shaped cookies with blood-red icing to the Coalition for Life workers who had taken up residence next door, nothing was considered sacred or off limits.

At first, my fellow workers' macabre attempts at humor made me feel physically ill. When I could, I would walk away without saying a word. Still, it was not enough for me to quit. As time went on, I found myself scoffing and even participating in their black jokes. When I look back now, I marvel that my mind had become so numb, that my conscience had slowly but surely been seared.

One day the nurse at our clinic called me into her office, where she and several other workers were reading a story about a young woman who had died. The article talked about her strong pro-life convictions. She had been a sidewalk counselor and had worked alongside her husband at our clinic.

While my coworkers joked at the dead woman's expense, I peeked over their shoulders to study the article. There were pictures of the woman and her husband praying together outside of our facility. She looked so happy, so peaceful. A deep sense of sadness came over me. The woman was young and newly married.

I was jolted back to the present when I heard the nurse say, "See? This is just proof that God is on our side. The pro-lifers keep on dying." Everyone started to laugh and make similar comments. I struggled to breathe and had to leave the room. In a daze, I hurried back to my office and shut the door. For a long time, I sat at my computer and looked up articles about the young woman. I searched for pictures of her and stared at her image on the screen. Nothing about her life being cut short was funny to me. In fact, it was tragic.

For a few moments, I allowed myself to feel and to think and to ask the questions that had pricked my battered conscience over the last few years. Is an alarm-system code that mocks the end of a baby's life or a freezer full of grotesque dismembered fetal parts funny? Was the death of a very sick, but also a very kind and spirited young woman something to kid around about? I knew the answer, and it felt good to say, even though it was only to myself in the privacy of my office, that it was just plain wrong.

But allowing myself, albeit briefly, to visit that place in my mind was a very dangerous thing. Instantly, I was gripped with fear. Was the cause that I had devoted my entire adult life to wrong? If so, could I stay? No. I was not ready to ask those questions or to face the answers. As I had done on so many occasions, I made a decision to ignore my conscience. After one last look, I x-ed out of the article and forced myself to return to work.

I am so grateful that God never gave up on me. That instead of turning me over to my sin, he forced the scales from my eyes and permitted me to see. Now that I am pro-life, I find myself interacting with that young sidewalk counselor's family at different functions. To be around them is almost too much to bear.

I take solace in the fact that God has given me the gift of a renewed conscience. The unrepentant sin that I stubbornly had chosen for so long had made me numb to the warnings of the conscience that he lovingly had placed within me. Yet, my heavenly Father, in his mercy, continued to reach out to me day after day and finally allowed me to see.

In the past when I would hear of atrocities such as the ones that have come out of the Women's Medical Society in Philadelphia, my response was to minimize the weight of my own sin in comparison to the ones that took place there. It was a way to ease the guilt and shame that still overwhelm me from time to time. Today, because the Lord has graciously softened my heart, when I hear of similar horrors, I whisper, "But for the grace of God go I."

I thank God for not allowing my heart to become so hard that his spirit could not penetrate it. I pray that even Kermit Gosnell and his staff would find the same redemption and forgiveness that I have. With God, all things are possible.

4

Daddy's Little Girl

A strange ambiance forms in the waiting room of an abortion clinic as the women shuffle in for their procedures. Many take a seat and distract themselves with their phones or iPods. Some flip through pop-culture magazines, hardly absorbing drivel such as which actress wore an outfit best. The ice is often broken by an offhand comment ridiculing the pro-life protestors that gather outside. Typically something along the lines of, "Those people are whack jobs", or "Don't they have anything better to do?" Snide remarks and nervous laughter follow, and the women begin to bond.

Unplanned pregnancy is no respecter of persons. Abortion clinic clientele are a true cross section of America. Girls barely into their teens and women nearing the end of their childbearing years, college graduates and high school dropouts, and women from all ethnicities and religious backgrounds congregated in our waiting room seeking to end the lives of their babies.

On the surface, their chatter seemed no different than the polite exchange of niceties that occur in any waiting room. The girls would chitchat about their jobs, boyfriends, and children. Invariably, the conversation would veer to what brought them to the clinic that day. The protestors outside, however peaceful, helped the women to see themselves as underdogs, and a sort of camaraderie developed between them.

Often they would share their stories, detailing their particular set of circumstances and explaining why it was virtually impossible for them to continue the pregnancy. The others listened and cheered them on. Each woman was assured that she was making the right decision, because if she wasn't, were they? Women who frequented the clinic would brush first-timers' fears aside with a wave of their hands. "It's quick and easy. You'll be fine."

The empty platitudes they shared with each other served as a defense mechanism designed to quiet the guilt and justify the decision they were about to make.

I would often glance out at the women in the waiting room through the glass partition as I buzzed about the clinic on abortion days. One by one, they were called back for the standard pre-procedure counseling and paperwork. The faces of the numerous women I sold abortions to over the years are a blur to me now. Perhaps that's my mind's own defense mechanism. There are, however, some faces that flatly refuse to blend in with the rest, faces that I still can see clearly when I close my eyes. One is of a sixteen-year-old girl with clear, pale skin and long red hair. I'll call her Lily.

I was immediately struck by her. Her face was free of makeup, she wore no jewelry, and her clothing was nondescript. Instead of playing on a phone or joking with the other girls, Lily clutched a book and studied it intently. I remember thinking that she seemed incredibly out of place. While many of our clients had a rather worldly way about them, Lily had an air of innocence. Her father sat next to her, his arm protectively around her shoulder.

As I walked them through the paperwork and counseling process, Lily's father constantly interrupted to ask if she was sure that this was what she wanted to do. Each time she answered that she was, but her yes seemed a bit more tentative. I did what I was trained to do when we sensed indecision. I ignored her hesitance and his obvious concern and hurriedly pushed through the legalities. Finally, her dad gave his reluctant consent and was immediately separated from her and herded back to the waiting room. The sadness in his eyes still haunts me.

I escorted Lily to the back room, and she stopped me as I prepared to leave. She asked if I would sit with her and hold her hand during the procedure. I was struck by how small and childlike she seemed in that moment. Her red-rimmed eyes were wide with fear. For a brief moment I visualized the stack of paperwork that had been steadily accumulating on my desk. "Of course I will," I replied. After all, I hadn't started volunteering in the abortion movement years ago to complete paperwork. I had a sincere, although incredibly misguided, desire to help women in crisis.

Lily changed into a gown and was on the table in no time. The reality of what was about to happen seemed to settle on her, and she began to weep softly. The anesthesia was administered, and she appeared to tolerate it well. In a matter of moments she was practically asleep. I sat by her side and held her limp hand, as I'd promised I would.

The procedure was almost over and as far as I could tell went smoothly. I breathed a sigh of relief for the semi-conscious teenager on the table. She looked so vulnerable lying there. "Just another minute, honey," I whispered. "You're doing great."

I was already mentally reviewing my to-do list, prioritizing tasks to determine what absolutely had to be done that day and what could be put off until later in the week, when I noticed an abrupt change in the doctor's normally stoic face. My heart sank.

"Ultrasound probe," he barked.

The doctor situated the probe on Lily's stomach and he, the nurse, and I watched the screen intently. I gasped when I saw that her uterus was completely black. I knew what that meant. Her uterus was filled with blood. Lily was hemorrhaging.

The doctor immediately suctioned what appeared to be a massive amount of blood, and within seconds it was filled again.

"Hemabate," he demanded.

The nurse sped out of the room and was back in seconds with the drug. I sat at Lily's side, clasping her hand tightly and silently praying. I knew what Hemabate was. This was not the first time that I'd witnessed a doctor frantically call for it.

I reeled at the mention of the word. It triggered a memory that I had taken great pains to bury. I closed my eyes and saw the face of another young and very troubled girl I had once befriended. She was the kind of kid who had no anchor. Searching for worth and a sense of value, she bounced from one bad relationship to another.

When she called me one day to tell me that she was pregnant, I urged her to abort and told her that I could schedule her for the following Saturday. Although she didn't seem sure, I persuaded her that this was for the best.

I doubted that she was even sure who the father was. I knew that she looked up to me and would follow my lead.

The following Saturday she showed up as planned. I performed all of her preliminary paperwork and counseling, as well as a full STD panel. Because she was my friend, I sat with her through her procedure.

That day was the first time that I had heard the word "Hemabate". Although my friend was somewhat sedated, she was crying out, obviously in a significant amount of pain. Although my recollection of the details are sketchy, I clearly recall her blood just pouring out onto the floor.

"Hemabate! Hemabate!" the doctor had yelled.

At the time I had no clue what that was. The nurse sprinted from the room and quickly returned with a vial. They began to pack something into her body, and continued to do so for what seemed like a very long time as my friend wailed and begged them to help her. After about an hour, the hemorrhaging, as well as her cries of pain, finally ceased.

Mercifully, my friend doesn't recall anything that happened inside the procedure room that day. I have never been able to tell her that she nearly died on that table. I couldn't bring myself to admit that my thoughtless coercion had almost taken her life, as well as the life of her baby.

The jostling of Lily's body snapped my attention back to the present. The nurse was spreading her legs as far as they would possibly go in the stirrups. I couldn't help but think how unnatural this seemed for such a demure sixteen-year-old girl. I held her placid hand tightly and watched in horror as they administered the vial of Hemabate directly to her uterus and then packed her vaginal canal and uterus full of gauze. It didn't take long before the gauze was stained crimson. It was removed and they packed her with fresh gauze. This happened over and over.

Lily started to stir. The effects of the sedation were wearing off. They gave her more. And more, and then some more. This went on for three hours. For three full hours she lay on that table. During that time they continued to pump IV sedation into her veins, far exceeding what is medically reasonable. Over and over they packed her full of gauze, extracted it when it was soaked with blood, and packed her again. Her skin, which was fair to begin with, was now a ghostly shade of white. The nurse asked if she should be taken to the emergency room.

"No," the doctor insisted. "We'll get it under control."

I had seen enough. I went to my supervisor and told her that this girl was in trouble. She needed to be transported to the emergency room immediately. I was stunned by her answer: "We cannot call an ambulance."

I didn't have to ask why. I knew. Nothing looks worse for an abortion clinic than an ambulance pulling up outside. If the pro-lifers caught wind of that, they would surely speculate, and the clinic's name would be dragged through the mud.

Meanwhile, Lily's father, who had been apprehensive the second he had walked his daughter into the clinic, was pacing the waiting room on the verge of full-scale panic. When Lily had made her appointment she had been told that she would be there for a maximum of three hours. It was now approaching five, and her father was barraging the secretary with questions about his daughter's procedure.

It was decided that someone had to go out to talk to him—or to put it more succinctly, to lie to him. It was decided that that person should be me. I took a moment to collect myself and rehearse what I would say to him. I wondered if he would detect my deceit. My hands shook and my skin was clammy. I took a few deep, measured breaths before turning the knob and entering the waiting room. Lily's dad hurdled toward me.

"How is she? It's been so long! What is taking so long?"

I swallowed hard and masked my own fear with a smile that I prayed didn't come across as forced. "Sir," I started, careful to keep my words from rushing out in a torrent, "I am so sorry for the delay. We had a procedure that was a bit more complicated than we anticipated, so we really got backed up. We are trying our best to get caught up now."

His shoulders fell and the crease between his eyes disappeared. "Oh, thank God."

He sat and smiled up at me. It was as if a weight had been lifted off of him.

"It won't be much longer. Thanks for your patience." I scurried back through the door and half ran back to the procedure room, hating myself with every step.

Thankfully, the doctor was finally able to get Lily's bleeding under control. Although it took a long time for her to come out of the outrageous amount of anesthesia that had been pumped into her, and she was undoubtedly in a significant amount of pain, she left the clinic that day, leaning on her father for support. Neither one of them had any idea of the nightmare she had endured that day or how close she had come to losing her life.

Her memory haunts me. To acknowledge that I had a hand in not only ending the life of her baby that day, but also covering up the physical ordeal that her small body endured, is difficult to bear. When I hear people spouting off slogans such as how abortion should be legal, safe, and rare, I think of Lily and countless others like her. Some weren't fortunate enough to walk out of the clinic and instead exited in body bags. Wherever she is, I pray that she has found healing and peace, and I pray that one day I will have a chance to tell her face-to-face how truly and deeply sorry I am.

5

A Special Place in Hell

As a former abortion clinic worker turned outspoken pro-life activist, I have the opportunity to share my story at numerous events around the country. I never try to waste an opportunity to share my experience in the clinic and how God opened my eyes to the evil of abortion. I was invited to speak at one of the oldest universities on the West Coast. I am always excited to speak at these types of venues. Not that I don't absolutely love speaking at pregnancy-center banquets. It is a remarkable thing to feel the loving support of those in attendance and hear how centers around the country are helping women in crisis choose life for their babies and continuing to provide for them long after delivery. I live for that kind of thing.

At the time of my invitation, the university espoused a liberal view regarding most social issues, but this did not deter me. These types of venues offer a rare opportunity for me to share my message with a crowd that, in large part, vehemently disagrees with me. Although it is scary, and I try not to let myself be intimidated, I know that my mission in life is not always to be preaching to the choir.

I arrived early to do an interview with a local television station. The chants of the abortion advocates could be heard from the parking lot.

Pro-life. That's a lie. You don't care if women die!
Our bodies! Our lives! Our right to decide!

I steeled myself, held my head high, and walked toward the building. As we approached, I noticed that although they were certainly loud and were doing a terrific job of making their presence known, it was a relatively small group that had congregated to protest my visit; I would guess between twenty and thirty. I paused briefly for a friend to snap a picture. I was all smiles and giving an enthusiastic thumbs-up—all the while with the protestors in the background, holding their signs and marching in circles as they chanted.

Sometimes, when I take a few minutes to allow my mind to wander, it all seems so incredibly surreal to me. A fairly short time ago, that was me. I know those chants by heart. I remember piling into a van with friends—all of us outfitted in hot pink and clasping signs that boldly declared to the world that we "Stand with Planned Parenthood" or snidely instructed the opposition to "Keep Their Rosaries Out of Our Ovaries".

It's not that I look back on these times fondly. It is hard to describe to someone who hasn't experienced it. The energy in the air is almost palpable. The atmosphere of camaraderie, of being united in a battle against a common foe, to continually shout those chants in unison with hundreds of others was intoxicating. To know that I was an integral part of something, that I belonged, seemed to fill a deep emptiness inside of me—a bottomless pit of longing that I now know can only be filled by God.

Looking back, I am simply bowled over by the irony of it all. There I was in my pink, waving my sign and screaming canned slogans until my voice was reduced to barely a squeak—all because I cared about women. I was proud to stand with my sisters and brothers who were also militant about a woman's right to choose when, and if, she would have a child. At that time, I was fully convinced that my feet were firmly planted on the side of truth. It hurt me to think of poor women dying from their attempts to self-abort with coat hangers or knitting needles—or having one unwanted baby after another because pro-lifers fought to deny them access to birth control and abortion. The abortion activists that I linked arms with were fighting for women. And we continued to fight because we loved women and wanted to protect them. That's what we told ourselves.

Madeline Albright, a staunch supporter of abortion, once said that "there is a special place in hell for women who do not help other women."[1] Although these days I disagree with Ms. Albright about most things, on this I think I can agree.

Live Action, a youth-led movement dedicated to building a culture of life and ending abortion, was founded in 2003 by a then fifteen-year-old Lila Rose. In 2011, Live Action executed a sting operation on a Planned Parenthood clinic in New Jersey. Their goal was to expose how the abortion industry often works hand in hand with those who use and oppress women and assists them in keeping their illegal and unspeakable acts from being discovered, and ultimately prosecuted.

Posing as a pimp and a prostitute, pro-life activists entered the clinic armed with a hidden camera and microphone. The results were chilling and delivered a one-two

---

[1] Madeleine Albright, keynote speech at Celebrating Inspiration luncheon with the WNBA's All-Decade Team, July 13, 2006.

punch to Planned Parenthood that left a mark. Still reeling, their powerful PR machine quickly leapt into damage control mode.

The hidden camera clearly shows the clinic's "counselor" listening and nodding as the pseudo-pimp explains that he and his girls are in "sex work". He adds that his girls, some as young as fourteen, often contract STDs and are in need of treatment. The counselor coaches him about how to get around the law. She warns against allowing the girls to state their true age on the paperwork and encourages having the girls say nothing.

"We want as little information as possible," she says.

She warns him to have the girls lie to medical staff about the ages of their partners. Knowing that most of the "pimp's" workers are minors, she even gives him helpful hints as to how he can get a discount for services at the clinic by suggesting that they say that they are students.

"Just play along that they are students," she says. "We want to make it look as legit as possible."

The "pimp" then asks how much recovery time his prostitutes need after an abortion. "I mean, they still gotta make money, you know," he says.

The clinic worker nods sympathetically before telling him that unfortunately the girls would need a minimum of two weeks before he could sell their bodies again. She does, however, try to help him out and offers some helpful hints.

"Yeah, um, waist up," she says as she gestures. "Or, they could be that extra action walking by."

I think, or at least I would hope, that folks on both sides of the fence were equally appalled by Live Action's findings at the New Jersey clinic. And in no way am I suggesting that this sort of thing happens on a regular basis at most Planned Parenthood clinics across the country. Although clinics within our affiliate had problems with covering up ages, at the clinic I directed I personally reviewed every chart. We would never have facilitated the sexual slavery of minors or offered a pimp tips to make his operation more lucrative while he begrudgingly allowed his girls a few weeks to recover from their abortions.

And yet, with all of our slogans and vows to help and protect women, I know in my heart that although our transgressions were not as blatant and egregious, we committed our own sins of omission that allowed women to continue to be abused and demeaned.

There was a woman that had probably been a patient at my clinic for ten years or more. I'll call her Diane. She was such a frequent flyer that we had to have four separate charts to accommodate her history with us. I remember that they were thick, worn, dog-eared, and falling apart.

Diane was a prostitute. We didn't know this about her because she donned stilettos, clingy minidresses, and fishnet stockings. In fact, the prostitutes we treated often came in filthy. Their hair was matted, and it seemed that they didn't have an opportunity to shower more than once a week. They often wore oversized T-shirts and jeans that appeared to be from the '80s. We knew that she was a prostitute because her poor mother, who often spent days on end searching the streets for Diane to bring her in for her STD screenings and Depo-Provera shots, shared freely with us. We all felt for the woman. She was obviously exhausted, exasperated, and deeply grieved by the life her daughter lived. She opened up to us. It was obvious that she needed someone to vent to.

She told us how shortly after Diane had started selling herself she had become pregnant. She chose life for her son, but never received any prenatal care. She delivered her child, unassisted by medical personnel, at a friend's house. I shudder to think what that must have been like for her. I have nothing against home births in general, but I don't imagine that this was the type of environment conducive to childbirth.

Unfortunately, when she delivered, Diane was suffering from an outbreak of genital warts, which were transmitted to her son. He developed laryngeal papillomatosis as a result and required frequent surgeries. My heart broke for Diane's mother, who had full custody of the child. She seemed so tired. Just tired and done.

Almost without fail, when we saw Diane she would be infected with one STD or another. We knew that she had a pimp. Typically she would have bruises all over her body, sometimes a black eye or a split lip or a gash in her arm. Many of us assumed that these wounds were inflicted by her pimp, or perhaps the culprit was one of her customers. But we never asked. A few of us were curious and speculated about her pimp. Was he a huge, scary sort of guy? Did he manage many women?

Women like Diane made me uncomfortable. The clinic's unofficial position on prostitution was identical to its stance concerning abortion. A woman had the right to choose what she did with her body. Period. End of story. We were trained to think that prostitution or stripping was as valid a choice for a woman as being a nurse or a lawyer. We were there to treat their recurrent STDs, abort their babies, and send them on their way. Never were we to "judge" their lifestyles.

Personally, I struggled with this mindset. I'd always had a deep and intense objection to pornography. I felt that not only was it base and vulgar; it demeaned, objectified, and exploited women. I hated how our society was becoming more accepting and pornified. Pop culture was always pushing the sexual envelope. The mingling of sex and violence seemed to be in vogue. Practitioners of sadism and masochism or swingers were subtly presented as valid alternate lifestyles.

I feared for my daughter. What would the world be like for her as a young woman? Was it even a remote possibility that she would grow up and meet a man untainted by all the smut? I am no prude, far from it. But even then, I stubbornly refused to believe that women such as Diane who sold their bodies to men for money were merely exercising their right to choose.

Although I was unsettled and confused about her lifestyle, it was a relief to see her bedraggled mother come through the doors every three months or so, a filthy Diane trailing behind her. *At least she is getting her shots*, I told myself. We were doing a good thing here for women like Diane. And for her mother.

Then one day Diane came into the clinic escorted not by her mother, but by her pimp. Anyone who knows me knows full well that I am not easily intimidated, but this guy would terrify Rambo. He was a giant of a man. I remember that he was dressed in a tank top and his arms were covered with tattoos, but his skin was so dark that it was impossible to discern what they depicted.

Diane cowered at his side, bruised and battered as usual. She seemed so childlike and frail in his presence. It was obvious that he had complete control over her. We got her in and out as quickly as possible that day. I watched as they pulled out of the driveway in a car that probably cost fifty thousand dollars. *Sex pays well,* I thought.

After she left the clinic that day, I turned over in my mind all the times she had come to the clinic with obvious signs of physical abuse covering her from head to toe, flashing like a neon sign. Although we often commiserated with her mother, we never showed any real warmth or compassion to Diane. She was treated like a child—a dullard that we were forced to deal with. At best, she was regarded with cold indifference.

We put on our hats of tolerance. "We accept your lifestyle." After all, it wasn't our job to judge her, right? We were there to protect women from all walks of life. That was our mantra. The day that her pimp brought her to the clinic, the realization that he was the one we had really been protecting struck me.

Every one of her black eyes or busted lips cried out to us, begging us to care. But we failed to even ask the most basic of questions because we didn't want to judge her way of life. She left the clinic that day, most certainly returning to a life of cruelty and endless days of servicing men for a paltry sum paid directly to her controlling pimp. In the end, I don't know what we could have done for Diane. Perhaps there is nothing that anyone could have done to save her from the life she had chosen. It's possible that she didn't believe in herself enough to realize that she could have been anything else. The years of abuse could have so damaged her soul that she would forever be ignorant to its intrinsic value.

However, I do know that we could have tried. I should have extended a lifeline to her. But I didn't. I wonder what Ms. Albright, having boldly declared that there is a special place in hell reserved for women who fail to help other women, would have done for Diane. I know that for my own sin of omission, for failing to protect women in crisis and as a result allowing those who profit off of their misery to continue to prosper, I had earned my own place in hell. And only by the grace of God am I rescued from that fate.

I thank him each and every day that, although I refused to act on behalf of women when they needed me the most, God rescued me from the pit and cancelled my own reservation in that special place in hell that Madeline Albright refers to. May he grant her that same grace.

6

Streamlining Murder

As an outspoken former clinic worker turned pro-life proponent, I often receive emails from uninformed people rabidly insisting that Planned Parenthood couldn't possibly be in it for the money. "After all," they protest, "Planned Parenthood is a nonprofit organization."

I swear my right eye twitches every time I hear that tired old lie. Don't get me wrong. It's not that I don't understand why people are ignorant. I certainly was, at least initially. It's difficult to blame them for blindly swallowing and then parroting the abortion industry's talking points that have undoubtedly been spoon-fed to them, oftentimes since kindergarten. The abortion giant has stealthily and successfully infiltrated our nation's public schools and created innumerable unwitting advocates for their organization.

Students for Life of America (SFLA) released a study in 2012 in which they interviewed 805 eighteen- to twenty-four-year-olds to gather their opinions and ideas regarding the abortion debate. They were shocked to find that 48 percent of them were uncertain whether or not Planned Parenthood offered abortions or not. Obviously, the reach of Planned Parenthood's strong propaganda arm is far and wide. The vast majority of people haven't a clue who they

are or what they do. Most believe as they have been told—
that Planned Parenthood is a trusted nonprofit health-care
organization that provides health care and much-needed
medical screenings to impoverished women. And they do
so because of their fierce and undying love of all women.
It has nothing to do with the eighty-five million dollars
the abortion giant cleared in 2008.

Mark Steyn, syndicated columnist and best-selling
author, says it best: "In America today, few activities are as
profitable as a nonprofit."[1]

In order to understand the abortion industry, it is necessary to comprehend fully that revenue, not philanthropy,
is the fuel that feeds it. The blinders must be removed
and the hot pink candy coating peeled back in order for
the public to come to this realization. And Planned Parenthood knows that there is no one better equipped for
the job than their ex-employees. That is why those of us
who have fled the industry and are vocal about the sins
we performed and witnessed there are the ones that they
most fear.

As an eager young woman intent on doing whatever
was necessary to advance to the next rung in the corporate
ladder, I was occasionally required to travel. Often I would
visit clinics within the state, and less commonly, I travelled
across the country. In 2008, I was sent out of state to a
private clinic that performed late-term abortions.

The purpose of these trips was onefold: efficiency. We
wanted to be better, faster, more organized. In the same way
that engineering geniuses labor to build a better mousetrap,

---

[1] Mark Steyn, "Komen has its awareness raised", *Orange County Register*,
February 3, 2012, http://www.ocregister.com/articles/komen-338772-planned
-parenthood.html.

my clinic sought to execute a more efficient abortion. I was there to watch how their clinic flowed, the order with which things were done, and when and how patients were seen. I was to take in every detail with one objective in mind: meeting and exceeding our own clinic's financial goals. I was also there to offer benevolently my own suggestions as to how they could improve their operation.

I recall being excited about this trip. The clinic I was to visit was run by a doctor who was very well known in the abortion world. I considered it an honor to go and work with him. I didn't wrestle with the fact that he performed late-term abortions. I don't remember thinking anything of it at the time.

I arrived and immediately got to work familiarizing myself with the practice. As I reviewed their policies, procedures, and billing documents, the reality of the clinic's specialty began to sink in. As I had trained my mind to do, I forced the truth into the periphery of my mind and focused on the task at hand. It wasn't until I came face-to-face with one of their patients that the grisly work this rock-star doctor and his staff performed hit me smack in the face and stubbornly resisted my attempts at rationalization.

I will call her Jessica. She was an attractive young woman with dark hair and ivory skin. Her eyes were ringed with dark circles and refused to meet mine when I tried to make small talk with her. Her swollen belly seemed almost cartoonish on her painfully thin frame. I couldn't stop my gaze from travelling to her obviously pregnant abdomen. It made me nauseous.

Snap out of it, I scolded myself. *That poor woman's baby has probably been diagnosed with some terrible syndrome that is incompatible with life,* I reasoned.

I was shocked to learn that Jessica's ill-fated fetus wasn't plagued with an unfortunate congenital disorder or chromosomal abnormality. It was, in fact, a perfectly healthy baby. I found myself studying her, picking her apart. Surely she must have some awful disease or mental diagnosis that made continuing with the pregnancy an impossibility. I was dumbfounded to discover that the reason Jessica gave for wanting to terminate her twenty-eight-week pregnancy was that she had recently broken up with her boyfriend. Newly single, she simply didn't want to have a baby.

Even then I wanted to shake her. Chanting slogans about a woman's right to choose abortion at any stage and standing face-to-face with a very pregnant woman preparing to do just that were very different animals. The solution to Jessica's problem seemed so obvious even to me. And it wasn't an abortion. I couldn't fathom why she wouldn't simply opt to deliver the baby and relinquish it to a loving childless couple. I started to verbalize my thoughts to a clinic employee when I stopped, my words trailing off midsentence. The argument that I was preparing to make was the very one that my fellow abortion supporters and I had scoffed at when made by those in the pro-life camp.

It is not your place to judge her decision, I reminded myself. *She is exercising her legal right to choose. Her reasons are her business.*

I chose to cling to my ideology and hold my tongue as I sat in on Jessica's pre-procedure counseling. Unfettered by any crisis of conscience, the director coldly detailed the three-day procedure for Jessica, who appeared distracted, even disinterested by the information. She sat with a faraway look in her eyes. Her hands awkwardly rested on either side of her. It struck me that most women in a similar stage of pregnancy would have naturally linked their hands around their bellies. It was obvious that Jessica was working hard to remain disconnected from the baby growing in the darkness of her womb.

The first day, the laminaria rods would be inserted into her cervix. Laminaria is a type of dried sea kelp that expands slowly as water is absorbed, causing the cervix to dilate. Next, digoxin, a medication approved for treating heart disease and used off-label for abortions, would be injected through Jessica's abdomen and into the amniotic fluid to cause the fetus' heart to stop. It can take up to forty-eight hours for the baby to die. The third day was procedure day. "Then it will all be over," the director stated matter-of-factly.

Jessica's affect was flat as she signed the consent forms and forked over the cash for her procedure. Before the ink was dry she was herded into a room where a syringe loaded with digoxin and laminaria rods waited. Fifteen minutes later the door flung open and she stumbled out. The nurse walked alongside her, rattling off instructions and reiterating what time she was to return the following day. "Take this just in case," she insisted, then thrust a large paper bag into her arms before ushering her back into the waiting room.

I watched Jessica leave the clinic. She seemed to be in a daze as she clutched the bag to her side and found a place on the curb next to the building to wait for a cab. Like most of the clinic's third-trimester patients, Jessica had travelled hundreds of miles for the notorious abortion-ist's services. Because she was so far from home, the clinic required that she stay in a local hotel that worked with the abortionist and offered a special rate to his patients.

"What's in the bag?" I asked, more out of morbid curiosity than professional interest.

"Do-it-yourself abortion kit," an administrative assistant answered as she shuffled papers. "It's just a biohazard bag and cinch, some gauze, and scissors. You know, just in case they deliver in their rooms."

"D-d-does that happen often?" I stammered.

"Nah," she replied with a wave of her hand. "Sometimes they go into active labor after the cervix is dilated, but they usually make it back here in time."

That night I lay awake in my own hotel room thinking about Jessica. I simply couldn't erase the image of her swollen belly from my mind. I so vividly remembered that stage of pregnancy with my own beautiful daughter—the unspeakable joy I had experienced with each kick; the way my husband and I would watch as she shifted positions, speculating if it was an elbow or a knee that moved across my stomach, joking that surely I was giving birth to an alien. It was such a magical time of anticipation and wonder.

Sure, there were moments that I'd been fearful and unsure that I would be able to manage a career and a baby. And the guilt that I'd stuffed away since my abortions continually ate away at me. Despite the fact that I'd dedicated my professional life to ensuring that abortion would be readily available to women, in the still and quiet moments, my decisions haunted me and caused me to doubt that I would be a good mother. As I tossed and turned I found myself wishing that I'd had a chance to talk to Jessica alone—before she had allowed them to inject the digoxin.

It's too late now, I told myself. *Let it go. It's none of your business. What's done is done.*

The next day Jessica reported to the clinic to have the old laminaria removed and new rods inserted. When they checked the status of her baby, they found that its heartbeat was still strong and steady. This didn't seem to bother the staff. After all, these things take time. Surely the digoxin would do its job in the next twenty-four hours, and fetal demise would occur. Jessica shuffled down the hall and stood at the appointment window for a moment to confirm her arrival time the following day and to review her pre-procedure instructions.

I glanced up at her from the chart I was reviewing and noticed that as she stood there she was absentmindedly rubbing her belly with both hands. She seemed even more distant than she had the previous day. Almost vacant. Instructions had to be repeated several times until she finally nodded and indicated that she understood.

"What a space cadet!" the secretary complained.

I stared at the spot where Jessica had stood long after she had left. I tried to imagine what it must feel like to know that the child she was carrying would soon be deceased—that she was the one who had sought out and purchased its death. I wondered if she had wanted to keep the baby before the breakup with her boyfriend. Deep in my heart, I struggled with her decision to abort a late-term baby. I had aborted a baby, but it had been during the first trimester, and I was able to justify it. After all, it was just a bunch of cells. I also knew that as an abortion clinic employee I had no right to interfere. I desperately wanted to stop Jessica and ask her if she really wanted her baby to be a casualty of a failed relationship.

For years, I had routinely facilitated first-trimester abortions at my own clinic, but witnessing a woman in the final stages of her pregnancy choose to terminate created such confusion and turmoil within me. Abortion was so much easier to justify when I could tell myself that we were simply removing an outwardly imperceptible blob of tissue. We didn't think of it as a life at that point. It was impossible even for me to negate the humanity of the viable baby that doggedly continued to cling to life in Jessica's womb.

Sleep eluded me again that night. I forced myself to return to the clinic the next morning. It was procedure day. *Get a grip*, I scolded myself. How would I ever continue up the career ladder of my affiliate if I couldn't stomach one woman exercising her legal right to choose?

The doctor, who rarely made an appearance at the clinic other than on procedure days, was there when I arrived. Initially I had been eager to meet him, but after a few moments of his company, I'd had my fill. He was somewhat attractive, and I could sense that he was a strong and charismatic leader. It quickly became evident to me that his ego was off the charts, and his anger was thinly veiled. That veil grew thinner still when Jessica didn't show for her procedure.

Mild irritation gave way to cursing and door slamming. He seemed extremely volatile, and I got the distinct impression that his staff feared him. Ten minutes turned into half an hour. The doctor barked orders, and the staff scurried to comply. They must have called her cell phone at least ten times, each call going straight to voice mail.

"Call the manager," he ordered. "Tell him to get her on the phone *now*."

The hotel manager did as he was told, and in a matter of minutes Jessica called into the clinic. I could hear her halfway across the room through the receiver. "I need to go to the ER," she sobbed. "I want to save my baby." The abortionist must have heard Jessica's end of the conversation as well. He snatched the phone from the nurse and demanded that she come in to the clinic immediately to finish the procedure. "The fetus will be dead soon enough from the digoxin," he insisted. "This is what you wanted."

"But the baby has been moving around all night," she cried. "It's struggling."

When he realized that he wasn't getting anywhere with her, he slammed the phone down. He grabbed his keys and ordered his nurse and assistant to follow him.

"Where are you going?" I asked.

"To the hotel," he answered. "We are going to convince her to come in."

I backed up against a wall and got out of their way. After rummaging around through a cabinet in the procedure room for a minute or two, the trio had packed a bag and headed to the hotel to "convince" a hysterical Jessica to come in and allow them to finish the job.

I stood there, leaning against the wall. I found myself praying for Jessica and her baby—that the doctor would find her hotel room abandoned; that Jessica was already on her way to the nearest emergency room. I wondered if it was even possible for a fetus to survive after a digoxin injection.

They'd been gone approximately thirty minutes when I heard the back door of the clinic burst open. It struck me that they'd be coming in the back door. In my short time there, I'd only seen the clinic's employees use the rear entrance. I instantly understood when I spotted the nurse and assistant on either side of Jessica, heaving her toward the procedure room.

Jessica's long dark hair was matted and glued to the side of her face by tears and saliva. Her face was a maze of red blotches, and her eyes were nearly swollen shut. Obviously drugged, she seemed to be making an effort to raise her foot to take a step on her own, but the nurses were impatient and wouldn't wait for her to coordinate her steps and dragged her instead.

The doctor trailed behind, ranting on his cell phone. After the nurse undressed Jessica and hefted her onto the table in the procedure room, he snapped his phone shut. His mood was foul, and his annoyance mounted with each passing moment. The staff did their level best to keep out of his way. Uncertain of what to do or where I should go, I decided to slink into the corner of the procedure room and sank into a plastic chair. I couldn't look away from Jessica, curled up on the table, moaning and cradling her swollen belly.

As the doctor approached, Jessica lamely attempted to roll off of the table. Whatever they had given her at the hotel, or in route, had sedated her to the point that her efforts were futile. She continued to whimper and squirm and do everything in her power to get off of that table. The nurse grabbed her arm, effortlessly restraining her, and injected an additional dose of sedation into her vein. Within mere seconds, Jessica's arm went limp and hit the metal table with a thud.

Under ultrasound guidance, the doctor administered another dose of digoxin through Jessica's abdomen. I had a clear shot of the screen from my seat. I saw the perfect outline of her baby. I witnessed it kick its legs and shift in an attempt to avoid the needle. The commotion was finally over, and the room was filled with uncomfortable silence. It took almost thirty minutes for the baby to die.

Because Jessica was unconscious, the staff members literally pushed on her abdomen to assist in the delivery. It was a boy. I remember being taken aback by how beautiful he was. The doctor snatched him, snipped the cord, wrapped him in blue paper, and tossed him into a red biohazard bag like so much garbage, then handed it off to a worker.

"I've taken care of everything for you," he hissed to the lifeless young woman lying on the table. "Now everything can go back to normal for you."

He ordered that she be transferred to the recovery room. The nurse unlocked the brakes on the procedure table and wheeled Jessica away.

I sat motionless in the corner throughout the entire ordeal, my mouth agape and brain scrambling to make sense of what had just happened. As much as I was in favor of what I considered a woman's sacred right to end her pregnancy at any stage, what I had just watched Jessica endure horrified me.

What would have been wrong with supporting her decision to attempt to save her baby? Was it simply a liability issue? Perhaps they were afraid of whatever complications a nonlethal dose of digoxin would have caused the baby. I sat for quite some time, turning these things over in my mind. Finally, the shock gave way to righteous indignation on Jessica's behalf, and I rose, fully intending to ask the doctor those questions and more.

I wandered through the clinic searching for the doctor. Finally, the receptionist informed me that he had stepped out for a moment. I felt myself drawn toward the recovery room. I felt a need to be with Jessica. I grabbed a stack of paperwork that I needed to go through before my visit there concluded, then pulled up a chair beside her and sat.

For the first hour she was as still as a stone—so much so that every few minutes I looked up from my work to make sure she was breathing. Eventually she began to stir and moan softly. Putting my work to the side, I placed my hand over hers. I wanted her to know that she wasn't alone.

As the sedation wore off, Jessica's movements became fitful. She thrashed against the bedrails, drawing the attention of the nurse.

"Jessica," she bellowed in a condescending tone, "everything went well. You are fine."

Jessica's eyelids fluttered and finally opened. She seemed frozen for a moment, her hands grasping the metal bedrails as she stared at the ceiling. When the realization of where she was and what had happened hit her, she started to tremble and shriek. Panic stricken, she locked eyes with me. I opened my mouth to offer her some words of comfort, but none came. I wondered if she remembered seeing me perched in the corner, silently watching as she begged for the life of her baby.

"You are going to be okay," I whispered. My words fell flat. I think we both knew that it was going to be a long time before she was ever going to be anything remotely resembling okay.

Jessica struggled to sit upright and began to scream. "Where is he? I need to see him! Let me see him!"

I jumped out of the way as the nurse and assistant raced toward her.

"You need to stop," the nurse hissed.

Neither the nurse nor the assistant made even the slightest effort to mask their annoyance and disgust. When Jessica's screams persisted, they threatened to call the police. Their cruelty and threats only fueled her panic. The doctor finally burst through the door. He spat curses as he lumbered toward her. Jessica was instantly silenced and physically shrunk from him.

"I just need to hold him," she begged. "Please."

He scoffed at her request, and when Jessica resumed her deafening pleas to hold her dead baby, he ordered the assistant to call the police and walked away. The complete lack of empathy on the part of the workers struck me. Instead of doing what they could to calm and console her, they rolled their eyes and exchanged snide comments.

Eventually the police did come. Ironically, they showed Jessica far more compassion and understanding than the people who made their living in an industry that claims to advocate for and serve women. Her cries could be heard even after the clinic door slammed and the officers escorted her down the sidewalk. She left that day with the knowledge that she was responsible for the death of her child, and with her requests to hold him and beg his forgiveness denied.

Unlike the rest of the staff, I was a total wreck. Every time I tried to focus on the computer screen or a document, my eyes would blur with tears. I felt my cheeks flush with anger when I heard the workers mocking Jessica. Finally, I grabbed some paperwork and headed back to the hotel. I had jumped into the abortion industry with both feet, dedicating my professional and personal life to defending what I felt was a woman's constitutional right to choose. But what I had witnessed Jessica endure shocked, appalled, and confused me.

I couldn't conclude my business at their clinic soon enough. The macabre scene played through my mind in an unrelenting loop as I finally flew home—the sickening thud of Jessica's limp arm on the table; the moment that her baby boy's heart ceased its fervent beating; the cruel indifference of the staff to Jessica's desperate pleas to cradle her dead baby just once. I had come face-to-face with the grisly reality of late-term abortion, and it was a far cry from the unfortunate, yet necessary, theoretical picture that had been painted for me by abortion activists.

The basis for my visit to the clinic was the abortion industry's unquenchable thirst for efficiency in abortion. Their expectation was that I would study the inner workings of the office and would return motivated to implement some money- and time-saving practices in our own clinic. I still firmly believed that abortion was a woman's sacred right, yet I couldn't stop thinking about how poorly Jessica was treated. I kept seeing her hugely pregnant belly and vacant eyes. I couldn't forget how she seemed to snap to life when she realized that her son was struggling inside of her and was suddenly frantic to save him.

As my plane taxied toward the gate, I quelled my uneasiness by reminding myself that at least at my clinic we didn't offer late-term abortions. Instead, our focus was on helping women who were fortunate enough to catch their inopportune pregnancies early. We dispatched the problem before their bellies had the time to swell and such drastic measures were necessary. Our objective was to educate women and arm them with the tools they needed to prevent unwanted pregnancies. We strove actually to reduce the number of abortions. This was a goal that resonated with me, and I bought into that lie hook, line, and sinker.

As an idealistic clinic insider, it was easy for me to believe the canned facts disseminated by the powers that be. When the nation's largest abortion provider claimed that abortion represented only 3 percent of the services they provided, I doggedly embraced that "fact". When anyone voiced opposition to my career, I shared it proudly. I was not in the business of abortion. I was in the business of providing quality health care to women.

The longer I was a part of the industry and the deeper I delved into the inner workings of the clinic, both medical and financial, even I found that "fact" impossible to believe. I knew what brought women to our clinic, and I knew exactly what "services" we were providing for them. The numbers simply didn't add up. When I went to my supervisors about this, I was instantly shot down. Instead of brainstorming with me about ways that we could reduce abortions, they talked of budgets and the need to increase our cash flow. The way we did that? Abortion.

"But come on," some will protest. "We have seen the numbers and the pie charts. Obviously abortion only accounts for a small portion of their revenue."

The short answer to that argument is that the clinics providing abortions are part of a wholly corrupt conglomeration that has mastered the art of deception. The long answer requires an understanding for how medical billing and coding works to grasp how the industry has pulled the wool over the eyes of the American taxpayer.

In retrospect, I see my business trips and budgetary meetings for what they were: an attempt to streamline the gruesome murder of babies in the womb. Women in crisis who were unfortunate enough to run to us were far too often manipulated into executing their babies under the guise of choice and convenience. I now know that the love of money is the root of all evil. As an organization that rakes in over one billion dollars annually, the abortion industry's heart beats exclusively for the almighty dollars made shedding innocent blood.

By sharing these stories of exploitation and abuse of women in the abortion industry, my fellow former workers and I are exposing the deceit. The eyes of the American people are being opened, and they are being shaken out of their apathy. The overwhelming majority consider themselves pro-life. Take heart, speak out, persist in prayers, and steadfastly continue in your pro-life ministries. We are winning.

7

Frequent Flyers

While the term "frequent flyer" is most commonly associated with jet-setting executives, those of us who have worked in the abortion industry also use the expression when referring to our regulars. Only instead of walking away with complementary pretzels and an accumulation of sky miles, our customers walked away with a human life unnaturally ripped from their bodies and a lifetime of psychological and oftentimes physical repercussions.

One woman comes to mind as an extreme example of whom we would have referred to as a "frequent flyer" at our clinic. I'll call her Angie. Angie was a tall, handsome woman with smooth brown skin and in her midthirties. She had a sharp wit, and we rarely saw her without a smile on her face. And we saw her often. When Angie walked through our doors for her ninth procedure, even those of us whose paychecks were funded by abortion shook our heads and said, "Really? Seriously?"

I recall being disturbed by Angie's levity regarding her procedures. Although it went against my own ideology, I wanted Angie to show some indication of remorse. I didn't feel that way about the numerous women who presented for abortions two, three, or even four times. But nine? That, I felt, deserved at least a slight show of regret or even a bit of good old-fashioned shame.

But Angie displayed neither. In fact, she seemed to regard her visits to our clinic as an opportunity to perform her improv comedy act. "Could y'all just xerox my chart and I'll fill in the dates?" she would jest. Once the paperwork was in order, Angie would attempt to banter with the other girls in the waiting room. "It's no big thing," she assured them. "I've done it eight times before, and I have no regrets." Although I couldn't help but like Angie, her flippancy appalled me. At that stage in the game I certainly didn't feel that abortion was wrong or sinful in any way, but women like Angie pushed even my moral buttons.

Most of our clientele required at least some level of coaching in preparation for their abortions: "Please remove all of your clothing including your underwear and change into the gown. Please sit up on the table and place your feet in the stirrups." Not Angie. She joked with the nurse as she made her way to the procedure room. She was completely casual as she stripped and changed into the thin gown provided. Devoid of self-consciousness, she would hop up on the table and plant her heels in the stirrups as if she were presenting for any gynecological well visit.

Angie even opted not to have sedation during her procedure. Perhaps Angie figured that she had endured the procedure enough times that she wouldn't have any problems being both physically and mentally present through the ordeal. And honestly, she didn't. Angie experienced the inevitable pain and cramping, but still she would continue to banter with the doctor during her abortion. "Be careful down there, Doc. I might want to have children one day," she would quip.

I remember wishing that she had opted for sedation. Her lack of remorse and shame made us all feel awkward. Over the years, I had consoled and held the hands of scores of women who approached that same table with much trepidation. Some would weep, their knuckles white as they gripped my hand until it ached. Others would clutch Bibles to their chests and mouth prayers begging for forgiveness, even before the abortionist had begun his work and when their babies were still safe in their wombs. Many times women would climb onto the table and remain limp and unresponsive during the procedure. Mentally, they were a million miles away. And then there was Angie.

She seemed proud of her indifference. It was obvious to me that she relished the reaction her jovial nature elicited from the staff and other clinic patrons. Angie never even attempted to explain herself. When we would talk to her about birth control and try to set her up with an appointment to explore the matter further, she would just smile and politely refuse with a wave of her hand. This baffled and infuriated me on many levels. I had entered this field intent on keeping it safe and legal. Even so, I was hopeful that through education and the availability of birth control we would decrease the number of abortions.

Having had more than one abortion myself, I had quite a bit of compassion and mercy for women who returned to the clinic more than once. I understood what it was like for a woman to find herself in the position of an unwanted pregnancy, not once, but twice, perhaps three times. But apparently my grace was not without limit, and Angie had exceeded its boundaries. Although she was extremely personable, by number nine her cycle of continual pregnancy and termination was stuck in my craw.

We were all relieved when Angie was wheeled into recovery. Finally she was dressed, sipping ginger ale and continuing with her steady stream of chatter that hadn't stopped since she had walked through our doors hours earlier. It didn't seem to matter to her that no one was really paying attention. As I was walking by, Angie grabbed my hand.

"Hey, do you mind if I see it?" she asked. "I mean, I've had it done so many times, I might as well know what it looks like."

I didn't have to wonder what she meant by "it". Her request, although it wasn't one that we received very often, wasn't completely unheard of. We were trained to strongly advise women against this, but in the end, if they persisted, it was allowed. I reluctantly made my way to the POC lab, located her thirteen-week-old fetus, and put it in a small dish.

I debated about how to arrange the pieces. Would it be best to throw them all together in a clump so that none of the parts would be recognizable, or should I piece it back together as we normally did to ensure that none of the parts were missing? There was no protocol on such things, so in the end I opted to piece the parts back together. Although my own eyes were still blinded to the true nature of abortion, because she seemed so unfazed, part of me wanted her to see. I wanted her to grasp what she had done nine times. Nothing could have prepared me for her reaction.

Angie sat in one of the recovery room recliners and leaned forward quizzically as I approached with the dish containing her mutilated baby. She was all smiles and seemed genuinely curious. Unceremoniously, I placed the dish on the table next to the recliner. "Here it is," I said. I glanced around uneasily, hoping that the other girls in the recovery room didn't follow suit and also request to see their fetal remains.

"Thanks," she said, her trademark smile still fixed on her face. When her eyes travelled to the container, she gasped sharply, and for the first time since she had arrived, Angie was utterly silent. A few moments later her entire body shuttered and gooseflesh was raised on her smooth brown arms.

When she reached out her hand to touch the baby, I tried to pull the dish away. She grabbed my wrist and stopped me. We were both silent for a few moments as she continued to stare at the contents of the dish. I stepped back and Angie fell forward to her knees, her fingers still wrapped around my wrist. The other girls in the recovery room began to take notice, and my discomfort level rose exponentially.

"I am going to go ahead and take it now, Angie," I said as I gently tried to pry her fingers from around my wrist. "Let go, hon. You're okay."

She remained frozen on the clinic floor. "That's a baby," she said, barely audible at first. "That was *my* baby," she said. Her volume steadily increased as a torrent of words poured from her mouth, words that made everyone extremely uncomfortable. "What did I do? What did I do?" she said over and over and began to sob. Some of the girls in the recovery room began to weep along with her. Some covered their faces with their arms or buried their heads in the arms of the recliners.

Fellow workers rushed to my side to aid me in calming Angie down. After a few minutes, it became obvious that she wasn't going to calm down. We couldn't even get her off of the floor. After discussing it hastily, we decided to drag her to the bathroom. At least the heavy door would stifle her sobs until we could figure out what to do. Angie flailed her arms and legs and her screams reached a fever pitch as we dragged her down the hall. We must have been quite a spectacle for the other girls in the recovery room. Finally we managed to place a still-panicked Angie in the bathroom and close the door. I suggested that she splash some cold water on her face and "pull herself together". Her cries, although muffled, were easily distinguished through the door.

"I want to take the baby with me," she begged. "Please, can I take my baby with me?"

I felt responsible. I never should have allowed Angie to see the fetal remains. My supervisor heard the commotion and rushed to the recovery room. She stood outside of the restroom with me, wringing her hands. Angie's pleas continued. I looked at my supervisor and shrugged.

"No," she said. "Absolutely not."

I sighed, lightly tapped on the door, and entered the bathroom. I explained at length why it was impossible for Angie to remove the remains from the clinic.

"I can keep it in the freezer," she whispered. At that point the bizarre reality of our conversation struck me. I was sitting on the floor of a Planned Parenthood bathroom next to a woman who had just merrily aborted her ninth child, trying to convince her that she didn't need to bring the dead baby home to put in her deep freezer. Sometimes truth is indeed stranger than fiction.

Angie would neither relent in her requests to take the baby nor emerge from the bathroom. Finally we called her emergency contact, her current boyfriend, and instructed him to come and get her. After spending forty-five minutes with her, he somehow coaxed her out of the bathroom. When they emerged, he had his arm around her shoulder. He was crying. They left our clinic without another word. We never saw Angie again.

After that, any requests to see aborted fetuses were flatly denied. We also denied access to ultrasound pictures. It scared us because it threatened our bottom line. If most women knew what abortion was, like Angie, they would refuse it.

The good news is that in America many ultrasound bills are passing, allowing women a glimpse of their unborn babies. The ultrasound exposes the lie of the abortion industry. It shows that we are not simply talking about tissue. It is not just a mass of tissue. This is a human being, with a beating heart, internal organs, fingers, and toes. It's not about the graphic nature of abortion. It's about the humanity of the unborn child. We must dehumanize the unborn in order to accept abortion.

I witnessed firsthand the dramatic and instantaneous transformation of a woman. Upon viewing her baby, Angie changed from a woman who had abortions like some women get manicures to a sorrowful and broken person, desperate to cling to what remained of her tiny child. As pro-lifers, we must persist in working to expose the public to the ugly reality of abortion in conjunction with encouraging abortion-vulnerable women to view an ultrasound of their pre-born babies. I'm willing to wager that America, like Angie, will then wholeheartedly reject abortion.

8

Sorority Girl

Since my retreat from the abortion industry, my personal stance on the plethora of issues related to life and abortion has evolved. The only thing that I was certain of initially was that I wanted nothing more to do with facilitating abortions. I wouldn't have gone so far as to say that I believed abortion was absolutely wrong or that I felt that *Roe v. Wade* needed to be overturned. All I was convinced of that day was that I was personally done with abortion.

I hadn't turned into a proponent for abortion on demand in a day, and my stance that every human life is sacred and deserves respect and protection didn't burgeon overnight either. Looking back, I realize that I had to undergo a deprogramming of sorts. For literally every objection to abortion, I had been trained to spit out Planned Parenthood's rebuttals point for point.

Although far less common than the rape and incest argument, ectopic pregnancies were something that we were coached to throw out when someone had objections to abortion—especially religious objections. If life begins at conception, and the pro-life movement seeks to protect life from conception to natural death, what then did we have to say about women unfortunate enough to experience an ectopic pregnancy?

An ectopic pregnancy occurs when a fertilized egg implants outside of the uterus, usually in one of the fallopian tubes. Questions regarding ectopic pregnancies are valid and merit answers. Sometimes those of us in the pro-life movement excel at slogan slinging, but when it comes to providing raw data and practical answers to the tough questions, we often lack. Your standard "life-begins-at-conception-so-take-that" type answer simply doesn't cut the mustard with this one. The Catholic Church has a very specific protocol for dealing with these pregnancies. And it isn't abortion.

The Catholic faith considers the sanctity of human life to be a serious matter. At the same time, the Church also recognizes that an ectopic pregnancy has zero potential to grow and develop and is one of the very few situations where the health of the mother is truly at risk. The stance of the Church is all about the intent of the heart, and because of this she teaches women to deal with ectopic pregnancies by removing the tube where the child is located. In this way, a child is not intentionally killed.

Regardless if you are Catholic, Protestant, or atheist, Planned Parenthood is not the place to seek assistance if you find yourself in any type of crisis pregnancy. A college girl I'll call Jennifer is a perfect example of a reason why.

Jennifer was a pretty blonde girl with an athletic build. She could easily have been the poster girl for any of the sororities at our local university. She came to the clinic with her mother, who was also pretty and appeared to take care of herself. They had an air of affluence. Jennifer's paperwork stated that she was presenting for an abortion. Judging by the date of her last menstrual period, we estimated that Jennifer was approximately eight weeks pregnant. However, when we performed an ultrasound, nothing showed up. Her uterus was empty. We then did a urine pregnancy test, which was positive.

We honestly didn't have protocol for this type of scenario. We probably could have done some further testing; however, that day, we were slammed. The instant that Jennifer had left the room to take her urine test, the nurse plopped another young girl waiting for an abortion in the room. And there were a growing number of girls on the schedule who needed the room and access to the ultrasound machine.

In short, we were simply too busy that day to worry about Jennifer's health and safety. After issuing a brief, yet stern, warning that she immediately present to the emergency room if she experienced severe cramping, we sent a relieved Jennifer and her mother on their way and went about the business of terminating the baby in the next girl's womb.

The following day, I'd barely set my purse on my desk when the phone started to ring. The woman on the other end was irate—so much so, that I failed to understand a single word she said. I held the phone a few inches from my ear and permitted her to rant for a few minutes. When she finally seemed to be slowing a bit, I interrupted.

"Ma'am, I'm having a really difficult time understanding you. If you would please calm down and speak a little slower, I'll do the best I can to help you," I said, my tone unquestionably patronizing. I had no clue who she was, but I certainly didn't enjoy being berated, especially first thing in the morning.

"It's a little late now," she retorted. "But you could've helped us yesterday instead of sending my daughter away to hemorrhage and die."

It finally registered who was on the other end of the phone. For a moment, I was speechless. I wish I could have said that I had been plagued by thoughts of Jennifer, that I had lain awake tossing and turning, obsessing about the pretty sorority girl that I had sent away. The ugly truth of the matter was that she hadn't crossed my mind since she had left the clinic the day before.

"I should call the paper," Jennifer's mother threatened. "People need to know about your negligence."

This certainly wasn't the first time that I'd been confronted by a patient or family member threatening to go to the media. More often than not, these sorts of threats were not taken seriously. In the heat of the moment people liked to talk tough, but when it came down to the brass tacks, most people would rather that the details of their crisis pregnancy or abortion not be local news.

No one could argue that Jennifer didn't have a rock-solid case against us. Shortly after leaving our clinic, the undetected ectopic pregnancy ruptured, causing her to bleed internally. If her quick-thinking mother hadn't rushed her to the hospital in time for emergency surgery, our laissez-faire approach to her health could have proven fatal for Jennifer.

At that point, I was still deceived into believing that Planned Parenthood was well-intentioned and existed to "provide comprehensive reproductive and complementary health-care services in settings which preserve and protect the essential privacy and rights of each individual", as the organization's mission statement promised. So I was shocked when my supervisor refused to comprehend the magnitude of our error.

I promised to have my supervisor contact her immediately. One of my roles at Planned Parenthood was to

manage patient complaints, and I had heard it all, often
from furious people using all manner of colorful language.
Other employees would often seek me out when there
was an issue because they thought of me as "unflappable"
or "levelheaded", but this call left me shaken to my core.
Because of our negligence, because we were too busy, a
beautiful young woman could have lost her life.

"Don't worry about it," my supervisor replied with a
wave of her hand. "Forward me her chart, and I'll make sure
it gets to the affiliate's abortion medical board for review."

Her nonchalance caught me off guard. I started to back-
pedal. Surely if she had heard me correctly, she would
grasp the gravity of the situation. I stammered, trying to
get the facts out again but was cut off.

"I understand. It'll be taken care of," she assured me.

The abortion medical board. It had a nice ring to it. I felt
more comfortable knowing that they existed. An objective
system of checks and balances in place to ensure that gross
negligence or incompetency were never tolerated; that patient safety and privacy remained uncompromised; that
the power the doctors and medical staff wielded wasn't
abused. In retrospect, I am astounded by my naïveté.

As much as I hadn't given her a second thought after
she had initially left the clinic, I couldn't force my mind
to concentrate on anything but Jennifer for the next week
and a half. Thoughts of her permeated every aspect of my
life. My heart leapt into my throat every time a call was
transferred to my line. I was hypervigilant with patients,
checking and double-checking their test results before
they were allowed to exit the clinic. I wasn't going to risk
another woman falling through the cracks the way that
Jennifer had.

When my supervisor told me that the board had made a decision regarding Jennifer's complaint, I was relieved. Exhausted by my vigilance, I was ready to put the whole business behind me. Clearly we couldn't deny that we had erred, and that our lack of judgment had dearly cost a young woman. I braced myself for the bottom line.

"Please give her a call, tell her that this is what we are willing to offer for her inconvenience, and let her know that she can pick up her check after three o'clock on Friday," she said.

She handed me the folder with the board's findings, turned on her heels, and walked away. When I saw the amount they were offering to keep Jennifer quiet, I laughed out loud. Six hundred eighty dollars. There must be some kind of mistake. I mean, the poor girl could have died!

"This can't be right," I called after her, hoping that they had mistakenly left out a zero. Or two.

"It's what the board decided," she called over her shoulder. "And don't forget to have her sign the nondisclosure agreement before you hand over the check."

"You want *me* to call her?" I asked, but she had already turned the corner.

The fact that she had delegated the task of presenting the patient with such a paltry sum raised my ire. I stomped into my office and slammed the door.

The inequitable reparation offered to Jennifer for her harrowing ordeal forced the abortion industry's dark underbelly into the light. Again, I had a choice to make. I could examine the facts and acknowledge that we had provided substandard treatment to Jennifer and follow that line of thinking to its logical conclusion: abortion clinics existed solely to make money off of women in crisis. Or, I could choose to turn my back on the truth and once again embrace the lie that I had become so comfortable with. We were helping women who had nowhere else to turn. By standing with Planned Parenthood, I was an advocate for women everywhere who simply wanted to exercise their reproductive rights.

Perhaps it was my pride, or the fact that I simply wasn't ready to replace the lies with the ugly truth. I chose to remain on the path of a career abortion worker. I took a few deep breaths and dialed the number listed in Jennifer's chart. I steeled myself against the verbal assault that would surely come after Jennifer heard the amount that the board had decided that she was due. I swallowed hard as the phone began to ring. Jennifer's mother answered.

The details flooded out. I knew I was speaking way too fast as I attempted to come across more matter-of-fact than apologetic.

"A check for six hundred and eighty dollars is waiting at the front desk," I said. "Jennifer will need to sign a paper stating that by accepting the money, she agrees not to discuss her experience at the clinic with anyone."

I pulled the phone away from my ear and waited. I could hardly believe it when Jennifer's mother sighed and calmly agreed to accompany Jennifer to the clinic the following Friday to pick up the check—which she did. I was stunned when she smiled and thanked me after I handed her the envelope. I sincerely would have preferred it if she had screamed and cursed at me. Her gratitude made me feel lower than an earthworm.

Oftentimes abortion advocates, or even hesitant fence-riding pro-lifers, throw out medical issues such as ectopic pregnancies as an objection to the crusade against the abortion industry. "Where would all of those poor women go for help with these issues if Planned Parenthood wasn't there for them?" they ask. I think of Jennifer—of how in our haste to abort more children, we showed complete disregard for her health; of the dozens of places in our area that Jennifer could have gone and received superior care.

Ectopic pregnancy is a dangerous and unfortunate type of situation, and women deserve more than an abortion clinic to help them navigate through the difficulties of a health crisis or unplanned pregnancy, ectopic or otherwise. Those places are out there. Each and every pro-lifer needs to be armed with the truth to refute the falsehood that abortion clinics serve underprivileged women. Do some research and educate yourself about the alternatives available in your area. Tell anyone who will listen that no Planned Parenthood clinic offers mammograms. Not a one. Local health departments offer far more services for the poor and uninsured than any abortion clinic.

The abortion industry claims that they provide high-quality, affordable health care to women, men, and young people, and that they are often the only source of family planning for a large proportion of the women they serve. For many years, I bought into that lie and made it my personal mission to disseminate this misinformation.

I was confident that I was on the side of justice and equality for women. I was wrong. Sincerely wrong. Jennifer deserved better. Women deserve better.

9

Little Brown Bag

Slogans are an influential tool for getting a point across. They can crystallize the message of a movement in a way that is both memorable and succinct. For ardent abortion advocates, their jingles do just that. They also quite effectively paint those who fight for the lives of the unborn as odious misogynists who endeavor to guarantee that hapless women are saddled with gaggles of unwanted children.

We have a voice, and we have a choice!

2-4-6-8, you can't make us procreate!

When women's rights are under attack, what do we do? Stand up! Fight back!

Over and over the abortion advocate machine would drone about women's rights, fighting for the women's right to choose. And as an impressionable and secretly post-abortive college student, I chanted right along with them. With the opposition fundamentally demonized, I was proud to enlist as a soldier in the army for the rights of my fellow women.

As I rose in the ranks from a health center assistant to a clinic director, my passion to protect a woman's right to choose only grew. I truly felt that I was helping my sisters in their time of distress. I considered it an honor.

One day I happened to be at the front desk when a girl entered the clinic. I'll call her Melanie. She caught my eye right away. She seemed distracted, disheveled. Her deeply creased clothes betrayed the fact that she had most likely slept in them. The majority of her dark brown hair was tied back in a ponytail, but large clumps arranged themselves haphazardly around her face. She clutched a brown paper bag to her chest.

"Could I ... Is there any way that I could ... I just have a question ..." Her voice, which had barely reached above a whisper, trailed off. Her light brown eyes briefly met mine before darting away. A smattering of freckles covered her nose and cheekbones.

"Come on back," I said.

Although I was scheduled to leave for lunch in a matter of minutes, I instantly felt protective of this mousy young thing. I wanted to make sure that she was handled with kid gloves. My burger could wait. Head down and shoulders hunched, she followed me to one of the counseling rooms. She sat and fixed her eyes, pieces of hair hanging in her face, and gripped the paper bag to her chest as if her very life depended on its contents.

"What can I do for you?"

She sighed deeply, lifted her eyes to meet mine, and shoved the bag toward me. Inside were four pills. The packaging read misoprostol 800 mcg.

"Could you please tell me how I will know if I need to go to the emergency room after I take these?"

My mind flashed back to my own medication abortion. I had thought that I was making the most sensible and noninvasive choice when faced with an unplanned pregnancy. I couldn't have been more wrong. I was sold a quick solution to my problem by popping a few pills, but what I got instead was physical and mental anguish beyond what I can express—the gushing blood and blinding pain; the fear that I was surely dying; the dread of living through another minute of the agony that refused to relent. I drew a breath and collected my thoughts. I got the feeling that, like a scared rabbit, Melanie would bolt if I came on too strong.

"Did a doctor prescribe these for you?" I gently probed although I already knew the answer.

Melanie hurriedly explained that she had gotten the pills from "a friend", and that she was planning on taking them at home to do her own medication abortion. Fortunately, she must have done enough of her own research to know that she was playing with fire. I was especially concerned because she didn't have mifepristone (Mifeprex), the first pill in the medication abortion regimen.

I did what I thought at the time to be the best thing for Melanie's welfare. I tried to sell her on the idea of destroying her child surgically as opposed to chemically. But she wasn't buying. She explained that she not only lacked the funds for a surgical abortion, but also that she didn't feel that she could wait.

Melanie began to fidget, and I got the feeling that she regretted seeking our advice. I made her swear not to run off the second I left the room. I dashed down the hall to my manager's office and explained the situation. She benevolently offered to provide Melanie with a properly monitored medication abortion at a significantly discounted rate. I checked the schedule for the following day and squeezed her in.

Although she seemed hesitant at first, I rattled possible consequences of attempting a medication abortion unmonitored, and she reluctantly agreed.

True to her word, Melanie presented the next day for her appointment. She signed the consent forms, received her instructions, scheduled her follow-up appointment, and was out the door in a matter of minutes. In that moment, I felt good. Fulfilled.

Because our clinic existed, Melanie would not have to guesstimate when and how to consume the abortifacient drugs that she had managed to scrape together from who knows where. Because women had the right to choose, Melanie was empowered to take charge of her reproductive rights in a safe and responsible manner. The cause I had proudly chosen to champion had protected and served this scared young woman, who obviously wasn't prepared to shoulder the burden of parenthood. These are the things that I told myself.

While I wished that I could have convinced her to opt for a surgical procedure, and I knew that her medication abortion would be far from painless, I truly felt that I had helped Melanie that day. I was giving her that voice and choice that I had shouted about until my voice was a mere croak. I wasn't going to let anyone compel her to procreate, and if her rights were under attack, I was going to be the one who would stand up and fight back. I was a virtual walking, talking slogan for the abortion industry.

That feeling of contentment and satisfaction with my vocation continued into the next week when Melanie returned for her follow-up appointment. Again, she was disheveled and tense. I was eager to give Melanie the "all

clear". But a routine ultrasound revealed a shocking discovery. The medication abortion had failed. Melanie's
baby was alive and growing.

The nurse and I exchanged horrified glances. As the
nurse apologetically explained the situation to Melanie, I
watched as her expression morphed from one of confusion
to relief.

Melanie rested her hands gently on her belly. Leaning her head back, she shut her eyes and breathed deeply.
Unsure of how to handle the situation, the nurse left
the room. Her muffled consultation with the abortionist could be heard through the door. I sat in the corner,
turning things over in my mind. What advice could I offer
Melanie? The certainty I'd felt about my involvement in
making abortion available to women "in need" began
to dissipate.

When the nurse emerged a few moments later, she had
a plan of action.

"Melanie?" she said. "What we are going to do is go
ahead and get you scheduled for a surgical procedure since
the medication abortion has failed. Okay?"

"No," Melanie answered. Her voice was faint, yet res-
olute. "This is a sign from God. I never should have done
this. I never should have tried to get rid of this baby."

"The medications that you took will have serious effects
on the fetus. You *have* to have a surgical abortion," the
nurse countered.

Melanie hopped off the table, collected her things, and
headed for the door. The nurse followed at her heels.

"Hon, if you allow this pregnancy to go to term, the
baby will have a lot of problems. It will suffer. You don't
want that, do you?"

"Leave me alone," Melanie finally muttered before disappearing through the door that led to the waiting room. The nurse's patronizing tone quickly changed to one of contempt. She slammed Melanie's chart on the desk and unleashed a chain of expletives. She was accustomed to dealing with numb, compliant women who allowed themselves to be herded along, offering little input or resistance.

Melanie was the subject of ridicule and gossip that day and the following week. Staff chattered about the girl who had walked out against medical advice—the girl who had refused to complete her treatment and who as a result was going to give birth to a "retarded" and "deformed" baby.

Multiple times a day over the next week I overheard the nurse on the phone urging Melanie to come back to the clinic for the procedure. She would rattle off the list of heinous conditions that her child was sure to have, if it managed to make it to full term: mental retardation, severe deformities, fetal demise, etc. I wasn't sure if she was being truthful or not.

Melanie wasn't biting. And apparently, after a few days, she decided that she wasn't picking up her phone either. I was torn. I still believed that a surgical abortion was the best option for Melanie and her unfortunate fetus, but with each slam of the receiver, I found myself rooting for her and proud of her staunch rebellion against the medical staff's assertion that she must complete the abortion.

If the abortion movement were to stand by its slogans, Melanie had a voice, and she had exercised her freedom of choice. We weren't trying to force her to procreate. We were doing everything in our power to make sure that she didn't, regardless of the fact that she clearly and repeatedly communicated to us that she did in fact want to keep her baby. I imagine that Melanie did feel that her rights were under attack. And we were the aggressors. Apparently standing up and fighting back wasn't her style. More passive in nature, she chose to halt our constant harassment by changing her phone number.

The treatment that Melanie endured from the clinic's staff after making the decision to continue with her pregnancy nagged at me. Disillusionment settled on me, and those slogans that I had so fiercely shouted began to take on a hollow and disingenuous ring.

I don't know what happened to Melanie or to her child. I pray that God's hand protected her little one from the toxic cocktail that we had given to end its life.

10

A Touch of Grey

I was raised in church. I attended Catholic schools for years. But as much as people associate Catholics with their pro-life stance, abortion wasn't something that was ever talked about in our home. Looking back I realize that I grew up in a virtual information vacuum when it came to abortion. In my home, at my school, and from my pulpit, the silence on the subject was deafening. I never really gave the issues related to life much thought. I now see that this lack of dialogue and education no doubt contributed to my vulnerability. Because of my ignorance I wandered down paths I would never have trod if someone had taken the time and energy to point me in the right direction.

When my mother did talk about sex, it was with obvious repulsion. Sex was dirty and disgusting. I even remember my mother telling me that she got pregnant while she was asleep. Despite her aversion for intercourse, she and my father managed to bring six children into the world.

Even in high school, I was always a conservative girl. Because of my brothers, my house was a wild place. For them, it was all about sex, drugs, and rock 'n' roll. Their lifestyle and the chaos it caused within our home bothered me, and I made the decision early on that I would live differently. I had no intention of getting mixed up in drugs and made the decision to wait until I was married to have sex.

I worked hard, and eventually I realized my dream of becoming a nurse. I landed my first job at a county hospital. Each and every day was full with the hustle and bustle of human suffering and conflict. Accident victims, women beaten by their partners, as well as less dramatic events such as gallstones and lawn mower injuries, were the staples of an average workday. Although it was busy and emotionally draining at times, I enjoyed my work. I was a good nurse.

I remember being shocked by a steady stream of young girls who sustained horrific injuries in their attempts to self-abort. I don't know if they chose to use knitting needles or have their husbands beat their abdomens because they couldn't afford an abortion, so much as they were scared and decided that they could take care of it themselves, and no one would ever have to know. Too often, drastic measures such as a hysterectomy were required to save them, altering their young lives forever.

This is absolutely crazy! I thought, alarmed by these girls and the serious injuries they sustained as a result of their do-it-yourself abortion mentality. I felt that these women needed a safe, clean facility with staff trained to perform abortions, in order to prevent these things from happening. Strangely enough, there was a clinic within a relatively close proximity of the hospital.

Not only was I able to sympathize with these girls; I empathized as well. I had secretly aborted my child—not with a knitting needle, but ironically inside the same clinic where I would be employed years later.

I worked at the hospital for fifteen years and enjoyed caring for patients and bringing them whatever comfort I was able. However, during a very rough time with my family, I was tardy several times in a row. This wasn't something that the administration tolerated, and eventually they let me go. I was devastated.

I worked odd jobs for a while and struggled to find my footing. I filled out applications online and submitted them to all the medical institutions within a reasonable driving distance. I was shocked when an abortion clinic and family planning center responded and scheduled me for an interview right away.

"You do know that this is an abortion clinic, right?" the director inquired.

I nodded and pushed down the flare of emotions that had been churning inside of me since entering the building where my child's life had ended. "Yeah, I know."

At the time, the clinic was looking to start up an intravenous sedation program. They were interested in me because of my extensive experience in this area. Although IV sedation wasn't considered a necessity for a surgical abortion, it certainly made the procedure much more tolerable, and it generated an extra fifty bucks per patient.

I would counsel the women during the sedation process before their abortions. Many of the women and their stories have stayed with me. One woman was there for her eleventh abortion. *Eleventh!* This disgusted me. One thirty-seven-year-old patient was having her seventh abortion on the same day that her daughter was having her first grandbaby. Her festive mood and celebratory attitude concerning her granddaughter's birth seemed morbid and out of place in an abortion clinic.

The faces of some patients have stayed with me longer than others. For example, an Asian girl who spoke no English presented to the office with an older and rather menacing American man. He didn't appear to speak her native language, but still insisted that all communication be routed through him. He filled out her paperwork. I thought it odd that he didn't even pause for a moment or attempt to ask the date of her last menstrual period. When he was done, he thrust the forms in her lap and motioned for her to sign.

The abortion industry claims to be a voice crying in the wilderness for women's rights, a bastion of modern-day feminism, yet none of us did as much as make a phone call to the authorities to report an extremely shady situation. Sure, we talked about it, about how uncomfortable his peacock-like posturing made us and how badly we felt for this gaunt little girl, who couldn't even bring herself to make eye contact. One of us even asked if we should call the authorities and forward them the address the man had listed on the form, just in case. In the end, we decided that it was better to leave it alone and mind our own business—the business of abortion. To this day I wonder what became of this girl, and I am ashamed that I did nothing to help her.

Unfortunately, I could cite a dozen similar instances of blatant disregard for the rights of women during my two and a half years as an abortion clinic employee. A young girl admitted under sedation that her father was the one who got her pregnant. And that this was not the first time. It was not uncommon for parents to trick their daughters in order to get them in the doors and then coerce them to go through with an abortion despite their desire to continue with the pregnancy.

The mistreatment of the women who came to us for help troubled me deeply, but perhaps the worst part of my stint with the clinic was the time spent with one of the doctors. He was the same man who had performed my own abortion years earlier.

I was shocked to encounter him my first week of work. To be in the same room with him practically sucked the air from my lungs. It was so intense. He didn't remember me, of course. Abortion doctors do not spend much time focusing on their patients' faces. He liked me. I thought he was disgusting. *I must be crazy!* I chided myself. *What are you doing?*

I spent quite a bit of time in the POC (Products of Conception) lab during my last few months there. I hated it. It was as if the clinic not only sucked life from the wombs of our patients, but from their workers as well. When I was in that lab, it was almost as if I could hear the suction machine sucking my own life away.

The doctors seemed to view the lab as a refuge. They would whistle or chat as they poured the glass jars full of remains into a sifter and rinsed away the blood as they searched for the body parts to piece together. I felt nauseous when an abortionist started talking to the baby he had just minutes ago dismembered.

"Okay, little one," he would sing, using the same melody that a new dad might for a lullaby. "Where is your other leg? Okay. Now, where is that arm?"

This is sick. I need to get out of here, I thought. Although I'd never really stopped looking for a job since the day I was hired, my search for employment intensified. I was desperate to get out of the abortion business, but I was also a single mother drowning in financial responsibilities. I felt stuck.

My superiors could certainly tell that my heart was not in my work. I was often reprimanded for spending too much time talking to the girls on the phone or in counseling. Their philosophy was "Get 'em in. Get 'em out." They would add more and more cases until some days the clinic had the feel of a production line.

The director frequently made a point to remind us that the phones were tapped and that we were to expect "mystery shoppers" to be calling from the main office. The purpose of these calls was to make sure that we were towing the company line. We needed to answer by the third ring. If a woman seemed reluctant to follow through with the procedure, we were expected to respond with canned pro-abortion rebuttals.

I got to the point where I simply couldn't do it. Could. Not. Do. It. But I was afraid of being unable to provide for my family, so I tried to be smart and not call unwanted attention to myself. I would privately share my own experience and deep regrets with girls who showed even the slightest bit of vacillation. If they seemed hesitant, I encouraged them to sleep on it and assured them that there was no need to hurry. Often, I would sneak into the bathroom to call the nearby pregnancy center to give them a heads up about a certain client that I was sending their way. I think I was subconsciously trying to undo the evil of my own abortion.

My time outside of work was spent desperately searching for a new job. I prayed and asked God to get me out of there. It seemed as if every promising lead turned out to be a dead end. Discouraged, I continued to drag myself to the clinic each day.

One day, my boss summoned me to her office. I readied myself for another scolding for talking too long on the phone, talking about adoption as an alternative to abortion, or slowing down the patient flow by lingering in the room with an unsure client. The truth of the matter was that she had called me in to end my employment problems once and for all.

I sat stunned as she rattled off a list of trumped-up excuses to let me go. Although I was actively and desperately seeking other employment, it still stung to realize that they had beat me to severing ties with them. As I sat there listening to her drone on, my cell phone vibrated in the pocket of my scrubs. Dumbstruck, I couldn't even answer it.

I was washed in an overwhelming sense of relief and optimism when I walked out of the clinic that day. God knew that I was paralyzed by the fear of not being able to provide for my family and arranged for the ties to be cut for me. And as always, he proved to me that he was more than capable of taking care of us. It turns out that the call I missed while I was being fired from the clinic was from one of the many facilities to which I had applied. Within a week, I was offered a job doing something that I was proud of.

What I wouldn't do to erase the years that I wasted at Planned Parenthood. I wish that I had flatly refused to make that first awful choice, which led to a succession of awful choices until my entire lifestyle had become something that didn't allow me to sleep at night. Pro-lifers often proclaim, especially through social media, that there is no way on God's green earth that they could ever set foot in an abortion clinic. They damn to hell those who have. I applaud you for your wisdom and moral fortitude. I offer no lame excuses, but I do urge people to consider the depth of deception that the abortion industry employs in order to lure people in, and the bully tactics used to keep them there.

I pray that my story can serve as a cautionary tale, as a warning to the fence-sitters who claim not to have an opinion about abortion one way or the other. I implore you to educate yourselves. Research abortion providers, starting with the founder, Margaret Sanger. Come to your own conclusions about abortion, but come to them. Have an opinion! I urge you to be diligent and proactive when it comes to teaching our kids about life issues. If we fail in this, please know that those in the abortion industry are ready and waiting to do so in our stead.

As parents, educators, and pro-lifers, it is our job to train our kids to understand that the issue of abortion is absolutely black and white. Abortion is wrong. All the time. If we allow any uncertainty to enter into the equation, our vision blurs and soon our moral compasses will completely fail to find true north.

A touch of grey took me from someone who personally found abortion to be distasteful but necessary, to someone who chose abortion for herself, to someone who facilitated abortions. Evil prefers small victories. It fights for gain inch by inch, because if we were confronted by it a foot at a time, we would surely recognize it for what it is and stand against it.

As C. S. Lewis writes in *The Screwtape Letters*, "Indeed the safest road to Hell is the gradual one—the gentle slope, soft underfoot, without sudden turnings, without milestones, without signposts.... Your affectionate uncle, Screwtape."[1]

---

[1] C. S. Lewis, *The Screwtape Letters* (New York: HarperOne, 1996), p. 61.

Any Reason Is a Good Reason

As the daughter of a medical doctor and a registered nurse, I grew up with a fascination for science and a passion for living things. My family was very involved in the Presbyterian church and was liberal, politically speaking. I remember them being quite supportive of Planned Parenthood and abortion in general.

Following in the footsteps of my parents, I became a registered nurse and started my career in the ICU of a local hospital. The thought of seeing the world appealed to me, so I became a travelling nurse and eventually landed in one of the Mountain States. This was in the mid-1980s, and at that time there was an abundance of nurses, and jobs were at a premium. So when I saw an ad for a four-day-a-week, day-shift position at a women's reproductive health clinic, I applied immediately.

I had never really given the subject of abortion a great deal of thought. I guess that I fell into that group of people who felt that I could never personally have an abortion, but supported the rights of others to do as they wished. At the time, the atmosphere in this particular Mountain State was very supportive of abortion on demand in theory, but fundamentally, deep inside, I think that most people had a distaste for it—hence the job opening. People might philosophically support terminating a pregnancy, but even in a notoriously liberal city, not many had an interest in dirtying their own hands.

I was extremely hesitant to share the details of my newfound employment with others. My parents and boyfriend at the time were aware and supportive. I remember telling someone that I worked at a women's health clinic and being horrified when they responded by exclaiming how wonderful it must be to work with babies.

The clinic where I worked was certainly not a facility of the same caliber as a hospital, but unlike many clinics with deplorable third-world conditions, overall it was clean and well run. The clinic's owner and abortionist was famous for his research into "safer, better" ways to perform abortions. In fact, he had authored several books on the subject.

The doctor's personality was a study in contradictions. He could be jovial and chitchat with the staff, and then turn on a dime and be nasty and abusive. I got the idea that he lived to provide abortions, but genuine compassion and concern for the well-being of his patients was completely lacking. There was no doubt that he was skilled at what he did. He was very proud of the fact that his practice had lower rates of complications than other clinics.

The doctor was also an environmental fanatic—a "Greenie", before the term was even coined. He lived for his regular jaunts to South America, where he "assisted" the locals in matters of public health. He wrote copious articles for scientific journals describing mankind as a "malignant ecotumor" destroying the planet as it continues to reproduce. With a worldview like that, it is easy to see how he was able to be matter-of-fact regarding his profession as a late-term abortionist.

The clinic was actually a warm, friendly environment of female employees, with the exception of the unpredictable and often prickly abortionist. I pushed aside my discomfort about working at the clinic and set my mind to being a good abortion nurse. I learned how to prepare women for procedures, set out the sterile instruments, and operate the suction machine. It was of utmost importance that a piece of cloth shroud the jar containing the "products of conception" from the patient after a suction abortion.

Gradually, I learned to help with "late cases", which at the time were pregnancies between sixteen and twenty-four weeks. These procedures were so much more involved, requiring ultrasound, two days of laminaria, and removal of amniotic fluid to be replaced with concentrated urea. After a few hours, the RN would listen for "heart tones". We had to be absolutely certain that the heart tones had stopped before the procedure could be completed. During my two years at the clinic, I was involved in the preparation for partial-birth abortions, but I never witnessed the actual procedure.

As I have since learned is the case with many ex-clinic workers, I had to fight to ignore and separate myself from my feelings concerning my vocation. This was especially true when it came to exceptionally egregious situations such as the woman who couldn't be bothered with birth control coming in for abortion number five—or a case that troubles me to this day and gave pause to even the most outspoken abortion proponents in the office.

This situation involved a handsome, well-to-do, young couple who presented to the clinic. The wife was obviously pregnant, and they appeared to be very compatible with each other. We all wondered what their story could be. I was not in on the initial counseling, but word rapidly spread through the clinic, and I remember not being able to shake the shock and disgust I felt when I heard their reason for choosing abortion.

This was a wanted pregnancy. The couple, who seemed to be well educated, was initially very happy to learn that they were expecting. Because ultrasounds were not as sophisticated or performed as often then as they are now, this couple did not discover until the woman was well into her second trimester that they were expecting twins.

What would be considered cause to rejoice for most was apparently grounds for deep thinking and intense research for this couple. They detailed how they had set out very pragmatically to investigate the impact that parenting multiples would have on their lives. They outlined how they had visited parents of twins to see what everyday life would be like and how it would alter their standard of living. In the end, they came to the conclusion that twins simply did not fit their lifestyle. Consequently they presented to our clinic to abort their healthy sixteen-week-old twins. And they did.

Up until this point, most of the cases I had been privy to were your typical six- or seven-week-type situations such as "Whoops! I am pregnant and can't possibly support a baby!" or "I am only fourteen and my parents don't know I am pregnant!" "She's just a child herself," we would say. Even most of these types of situations were easier to justify, although most of us would readily admit to struggling with them emotionally.

The same questions scrolled through my mind like credits on a marquee on opening night. Where was the line? At what point would someone in the industry stand up and say, "No! That isn't a good enough reason to abort your baby." Even individuals who identify as pro-life tend to want to classify certain situations as valid reasons for abortion. We've all heard people proclaim themselves to be against abortion except in cases of rape or incest.

The execution of this chillingly practical young couple's unborn twins taught me that in the abortion business, there is no line. As long as the business is profiting, there will never be a reason too heinous to end the life of a baby at the request of its mother.

Although I still didn't feel strongly against abortion, after two years of employment at the clinic I decided I'd had my fill and called it quits. I left on good terms and kept in touch with some of my coworkers for years after. My next career was at a level-three neonatal intensive care unit (NICU) for premature infants. I absolutely loved this work! I wholeheartedly dedicated myself to nurturing precious preemies, some of whom I might have helped terminate as part of my prior employment. While it is undoubtedly difficult for someone who has not been involved in the abortion industry to understand, even though I had become devoted to helping these little ones fight to stay alive, the irony of it all still had not settled on me. The system of self-denial was still too strong.

As my life progressed, I found myself occasionally listening to Christian radio. Some of it I enjoyed and agreed with. But when James Dobson, the founder of Focus on the Family, would come on, I would get so irritated— especially when he would go on and on about the intrinsic value and sacredness of life, both born and unborn.

Oh, how he grated me! After all, he was a man. How could he possibly understand what it was like to be trapped

in an unwanted pregnancy? In addition to my employment at a late-term abortion clinic, I had by that time
accompanied my sister-in-law and also a good friend to
their abortions because it was the "wrong time" for them.
To hear this man blithering on and on about the sanctity
of unborn life, it struck a nerve in me. In hindsight, I see
that our great God was gently turning my heart.

I married an amazing man, and shortly after we wel-
comed our first daughter. It was through experiencing
motherhood that I realized how indescribably precious
being a parent is. I remember feeling excited, scared, and
nervous when I held my baby girl and discovered that I
was one of *them*! I was pro-life! It dawned on me that
the formerly "valid" reasons for abortion suddenly held no
merit to me at all.

I still deal with crushing guilt for my participation in
the abortion industry, as well as sorrow for the workers
who are either hardened or blinded and continue with
this evil work. I am so thankful that I have been forgiven
by Jesus, but my past will forever be a sad burden on my
heart that continually motivates me to work toward creat-
ing a world where unborn life is treasured. I hope that by
sharing my story and through Abby's unique ministry to
abortion workers, we can work together toward this goal.
God is so good!

12

Fetuses: Wanted, Dead or Alive

I grew up in a denomination steeped in legalism. I mean, we loved everyone and treated folks with the hospitality that we Texans are known for, but at the same time we were pretty sure that we were the only ones going to heaven. All those people who danced, smoked, played cards, had sex, got pregnant, and especially had abortions were going straight to hell.

Because of my love for people and my desire to help them live healthy lives, I attended a local university to pursue my dream of becoming a nurse practitioner. I eventually graduated, found a job that I enjoyed, and settled into married life with children. Because of an unfortunate situation in my family, I was forced to relocate to another city overnight. Suddenly, I was jobless and scared.

I poured over the local newspapers in my new city and discovered that positions for nurse practitioners were scarce. I began to panic. When I saw that a nearby family planning clinic was seeking someone with my qualifications to run their clinic, I was wary. I was also desperate, so I made the call. I was told that this clinic did not perform abortions and that I would be in charge of family planning and STD screenings as well as pregnancy testing and counseling for pregnant girls. My fears were put to rest. I could handle that. I knew that I wanted nothing to do with abortions, so this seemed like a perfect fit. Looking back, I see how naïve I was to take them at their word.

Because the clinic was in close proximity to a large university, most of my time was consumed by the testing and treatment of college students for STDs and urinary tract infections. I also handed out birth control like candy from a Pez dispenser and performed routine pill checks.

My first few months there were a whirlwind. I had a relatively heavy patient load and concentrated on learning the ropes. Over time, I began to notice several things that deeply concerned me. For example, I looked high and low for information on local adoption agencies that I could refer pregnant women to, but I never did find it. When I asked my coworkers about this, they would give me vague answers, such as that they would "check into it". I tired of waiting and grabbed some adoption brochures from my church to hand out to women who had positive pregnancy tests. I also brought in pens advertising my church to hand out to my young clients, which the other nurse practitioner curtly ordered me to stop.

Another thing that I noticed over time was the miniscule number of women with positive pregnancy tests who were brought back for me to examine. I was aware of the considerable amount of pregnancy tests that our clinic was going through, and the small fraction of girls that I was seeing seemed oddly disproportionate.

I started to pay close attention to what was going on at the front desk. I noticed something that I hadn't picked up on before. Whenever a girl came in and asked for a pregnancy test, she was given a card. This card asked the woman, if she were to have a positive pregnancy test that day, how she would choose. There were boxes for her to check indicating whether she would choose abortion, adoption, or continuation of the pregnancy.

One would have to understand the fragile emotional state of many women facing a crisis pregnancy to comprehend the way that these cards pushed these women toward abortion. It was asking them to make a permanent decision based on something that was still unknown. By having them check a box to determine the fate of their babies before they even knew if they were pregnant, these women were making their decisions based solely on fear. They hadn't even been allowed to have a few minutes to allow the reality of their situations to sink in before they were asked to make a decision.

Still, this didn't explain to me why I was seeing so few patients with positive pregnancy tests. It wasn't until I overheard one of the front desk girls on the phone with another clinic in our vicinity that I understood the sinister truth. When a woman indicated on her card that she was abortion-minded prior to finding out the results of her test, the front desk girls would hold the card. If the test indicated that she was pregnant, instead of sending her back to me (the nurse practitioner), the receptionist would immediately call a clinic that performed abortions and schedule an appointment for her. I was livid. I wanted the opportunity to present these women with options; to encourage them to think about what they were doing and not make any rash and irreversible decisions; to let them know that they were not alone and that there were organizations that sought nothing more than to support them and help them choose life for their babies.

I seriously started to question where I was and what I was doing. But as a single working mom at the time, I felt that it would have been impossible to quit my job without having another one lined up. So once again, I scoured the papers and sent my résumé during my free time and continued seeing patients at the clinic. The unease I felt about my job mounted with each passing day.

One day, the receptionist called to let me know that they were sending a patient back for me to see immediately. According to her chart, she was about twenty weeks along and had been experiencing some heavy bleeding.

This woman seemed tired and was obviously in distress. She was desperately concerned about her unborn baby. She had two young children in tow, and it took a few minutes to get them settled and occupied with coloring so that I could examine her. I was instantly concerned for both the woman and her baby.

I remembered that I had a Doppler machine in my car that I had used when I worked as a midwife. I ran out, grabbed it, and dashed back to my patient. We both leaned in and listened intently for the rapid beating of the fetus' heart. An awful silence filled the room. Nothing. There was no heartbeat. I grasped the shaking hand of my patient and explained to her through tears that she was experiencing fetal demise. For whatever reason, her baby's heart had ceased to beat.

I instructed her to go straight to the emergency room. My own protocol as a nurse practitioner, and certainly what I had learned in school, dictated that if it was discovered that heart tones were negative, the mother would be induced and would deliver the dead baby. The poor woman was shell-shocked. She walked out of the clinic, a child on either side of her grasping her hand, and headed to the hospital. She assured me that someone would meet her there. I called the hospital to check on her a day or so later and was connected to her room. Her baby had died, but she seemed to be handling it well and was genuinely happy to hear from me. I felt in this instance that I had at least been able to provide this patient with some level of comfort, which was a welcome change from prescribing drugs for STDs and handing out birth control.

A few days later, the director of the affiliate stormed into my office.

"Who do you think you are using a Doppler machine in this clinic to try to let a woman hear a heartbeat?"

I knew exactly who she was talking about, but I was stung by the harsh, accusatory tone she had taken with me. I didn't understand why she would be so offended by my actions. After all, weren't we a "women's health-care center"?

"You mean the woman who was twenty weeks with fetal demise?" was all that I could think to say.

"Don't lie," she hissed. "We did not issue that piece of equipment or authorize you to use it. We do not use Doppler machines here because we do not want to sway the opinions of our patients."

I was dumbstruck. She was attacking me for doing what I knew to be the best thing for my patient. And I knew now that swaying every pregnant patient toward abortion was exactly what they aimed to do. Just when I was readying myself to reply, she changed her line of interrogation.

"Why didn't you send this patient to our abortion facility?" she asked.

"If I would have sent her there, the doctor would have done an ultrasound and told her that her baby was dead," I responded.

"Absolutely not," she replied. "By the time we would do the ultrasound, we would already have permission to do the abortion. The only purpose of the ultrasound is to size the fetus so we know how much to charge and what type of procedure to do."

I sat there. Reeling. I could hardly comprehend what she was saying, let alone come up with some form of intelligent response. I had nothing.

"It's not our business to tell them if it is alive or dead, twins or triplets," she finally said before she bolted from my office.

I rested my forehead on my desk and tried to focus on breathing. I was afraid that I would projectile vomit. What had I gotten myself into? I could no longer justify working at the clinic because we didn't perform abortions on site. I was earning money from an organization that was happy to profit off of dead babies. Of course, intellectually I knew that they snuffed out the lives of babies all the time. For some reason, the thought that they would knowingly allow a woman whose baby had already died to live the rest of her life thinking that she had aborted her living baby seemed even more heinous.

I told my boss that I was having a difficult time dealing with the job and I needed some time. I intensified my job search, expanding the area in which I was willing to travel and the scope of position that I was willing to accept.

When I did return to work, I was told that I would no longer be the nurse practitioner in charge of the clinic, which was fine with me. I wanted out, and it was just a matter of finding something, anything, that would provide for my family. I noticed that for the next two to three weeks, a nurse or receptionist would follow me wherever

I went. Suddenly, it occurred to me that they were spying. They were trying to catch me not washing my hands between patients or not wearing gloves. The atmosphere in the clinic had become toxic for me. I had challenged their ideology, and they weren't going to have it. I realized that they weren't going to rest until they had cause to fire me or I quit.

Directly across the street from my clinic there was a Pregnancy Resource Center (PRC). When I decided that I could not take being in that awful place for one more moment, I marched across the street and just charged in. I stopped at the front desk and announced, "I am the nurse practitioner for the clinic across the street, and I have just been busted for being pro-life." I burst into tears.

The women behind the counter stared at me. They looked at each other and then back to me. I watched as smiles crept across their faces. One of them handed me a tissue, and they sat quietly while I got myself together.

"Honey," the older woman of the two started in a calm, reassuring voice, "we've been getting so many referrals the last few months that we were sure that there was a plant at the clinic!"

I thought back to the few patients whom I had seen over the course of my employment at this abortion clinic, the ones who had indicated on their forms that they would want to keep their babies. I hadn't thought twice about referring them to the PRC across the street.

At the time, it hadn't occurred to me that we were in competition with them. I had naïvely thought that both abortion clinics and PRCs existed to assist women in need. I know how crazy this sounds to most people who have a clue about the industry and who they are, but at the time it was absolutely true. No one understands the power of marketing more than the abortion machine. In the same way that Americans associate cheap auto insurance with a cute talking gecko, the abortion giant has softened its image and established itself as a "mainstream women's health-care provider" through consistent and repetitive advertising. The organization has succeeded in white-washing its reputation to the point that many Christians do not even believe that they perform abortions.

Those sweet women at the PRC across from my former clinic took me in the back, surrounded me with love and acceptance, and prayed with me. *Oh God!* I thought. *What's next?*

It has been far from easy being a pro-life nurse practitioner specializing in women's health. I have job-hopped a lot since leaving the clinic. I was fired from one job because I refused to implant abortion-causing IUDs. Despite all of the uncertainty, and financial as well as emotional ups and downs, I can tell you this: it was worth it. Leaving this corrupt industry is absolutely worth it. I am so thankful for Abby's organization And Then There Were None (ATTWN) for helping people like me to find the courage and resources to leave. Most of all, I am thankful for God, who is gracious to forgive and has been with me every step of the way.

13

All in a Day's Work

We've all had them: one of *those days*, the type of day that causes us to seek refuge in the safety of our homes, curl up in a favorite chair with our fuzzy blankets, and pretend that tomorrow will never come; that we won't have to deal with a coworker's passive-aggressive behavior, hear the latest chapter in the never-ending drama of so-and-so's life, or endure another lecture from an unreasonable and out-of-touch supervisor.

During my years at the abortion clinic, I had more than my share of *those days*, for all of the aforementioned reasons and more. I mean, let's face it. I worked with almost exclusively women, and where there are women, there are issues. Gossip, slander, jealousy, and general cattiness were simply par for the course. But it usually wasn't the estrogen-soaked work environment that fueled my bad days. It was the dismembered body parts of the babies that really got to me after a while.

The POC (Products of Conception)—or babies, as I now like to call them—lab is a horrific place full of unspeakable gore. I know that now. And the higher-ups in the abortion industry know it too. As is the case with any atrocity, the perpetrators must whitewash their evil acts and slowly draw their unwitting accomplices in by somehow convincing them that evil is good—that even if an act is distasteful, the end justifies the means.

I believe that there is no better example of this than the hundreds of abortion clinics across the United States, each one of them with their own POC lab where workers casually converse as they piece together the torn limbs of dead babies like macabre puzzles.

As is the case with so many things that I said and did during my years in the abortion industry, I wish I could tell you that my moral compass found true north the first time that I encountered the mutilated body of a tiny human. Unfortunately, quite the opposite is true.

It is the practice of many clinics to shelter their new employees from the bloody reality of abortion for as long as possible. Most are started with innocuous clerical tasks such as answering the phones, entering data, and scheduling appointments. Slowly they are transitioned into the POC lab.

This wasn't the way my affiliate operated. They held to more of a "sink or swim" type of philosophy. New hires were asked if they had any problem working in a lab, which usually didn't raise any questions or objections. Before they could say *Vagina Monologues*, fresh young abortion idealists found themselves standing over a dish full of death. And it was their job to piece the body back together to make sure that the abortionist had "gotten it all". By throwing the newbies into the trenches of the POC lab, the "weak" ones were weeded out; the ones who managed to stomach it the first time or two promptly toughened up.

My first time in the POC lab was as close to an out-of-body experience as I have ever come. I had been at the clinic for several months. My boss was assembling the babies, and she wanted to train me how to do it. She motioned me over and indifferently started to explain the process to me.

"What you need to do is to make sure that none of the parts are missing," she said.

I walked over and my eyes fixed on the glass dish on the table in front of her. It contained the remains of a twelve-week-old baby.

Nothing would make me happier than to be able to tell you that I was utterly shocked and horrified by the sight of that dead little one, that at that moment I made my exodus from the bloody business of abortion and pledged my allegiance to the fight for life. But if I am being brutally honest, I have to admit that I was almost intrigued by that tiny twelve-week-old aborted human in the dish.

My boss droned on about the best and most efficient way to reassemble the products of conception and the proper way to document each one, verifying that the abortionist "got it all". I couldn't hear her. I was mesmerized. Of course, I had seen the graphic signs that the pro-lifers liked to hold up as they screamed at the abortion-minded women as they were escorted into our building.

However, we were always taught that those images were not legit. They were falsified by anti-choice radicals in an attempt to sway public opinion. We were taught that a first-trimester abortion resembled nothing more than a blood clot, and that the visuals used by pro-lifers showing almost fully formed tiny fetuses were doctored. They had to lie to support their arguments. Science was on our side.

I wonder now if I never questioned this because not only did I work in the abortion industry, but I had also had several abortions myself. It was so much easier to accept the fact that I had removed a clot of blood from my uterus that had the *potential* to become a baby than to think that I had hired a hit man to end the life rapidly growing in my womb. The only explanation I have now for my lack of emotion toward what I witnessed day in and day out at work is that the scales had not yet been removed from my eyes. I was willfully blind, and it was all in a day's work.

I remember feeling like I was outside of myself as I watched my fingers grab for the tweezers. I don't even remember making a conscious choice to pick them up. I closely inspected the tiny parts, full of awe and wonder.

"Wow. It's a miracle, isn't it?" I mumbled to my boss. "It's like we start out like this and end up like we are now."

My boss laughed, which snapped me out of my trance and got my attention. She stood there, hands on hips, and said, "I knew you were the one."

I stood there, tweezers in hand, confused. "The one for what?"

"You are the only person that I've ever brought back here that hasn't gotten all emotional. You are the one who will take over this affiliate."

As I walked out of the lab that day a sick pride welled up inside of me. I was certain that I would die a dedicated clinic employee. It felt good to know that I was the only one who hadn't cracked and shown weakness at the sight of an aborted fetus. I was more pragmatic than the rest. A realist. I could be trusted. I was "the one". Of course, now I know that not only was she appealing to my unrelenting desire to be accepted and needed, but that my ego was out of control.

Several years later, we went through a brief staffing shortage at the clinic and we were all stretched thin. We asked another clinic in our affiliate if any of their workers would like to come in on our abortion days to help us out. A family planning counselor agreed. She had been with the chain of abortion clinics for about five years.

Most people think it is a safe assumption that if someone has been involved in the abortion industry day in and day out for that amount of time, they have a fairly good idea what abortion looks like. People who work in dental offices, even in clerical positions, usually have a working knowledge of basic dental procedures and what they entail. The abortion industry is not so straightforward. This woman had no idea what she was getting into.

When she was tasked to piece together the remains of a sixteen-week-old baby, she cracked. Over her years of employment with the clinic, that woman had undoubtedly sold countless abortions to women in crisis. She knew how to answer their questions. "Will my baby feel anything?" "What does it look like now?" "Will it hurt?" She had spent years in the abortion industry, but a few short seconds in the POC lab was all it took to send her flying out the door, never to return.

I will always remember the panic in her voice as she ran down the hall. "It's still alive," she shrieked.

I rolled my eyes, annoyed at her weakness, and headed into the lab to clean up her mess and get the job done. Most babies come out in pieces. But occasionally, they will come out almost whole. This particular baby's head, torso, and arms were still intact. The legs were ripped off.

There was movement, but only for a moment. I accounted for the parts, estimated its gestational age based on a chart, and moved on to the next one.

I can't explain why seeing that doomed and dismembered little one in the dish that day didn't change me—or the many times before or after that I witnessed the same thing. God's timing and ways are mysterious.

There continues to be much debate about what abortion looks like. Have pro-lifers doctored pictures in their zeal to prove to the world that the unborn are in fact human, or exaggerated the gestation age? Yes. Do abortion advocates constantly lie about the realities of babies' growth and development? Absolutely. I have come to the realization that it doesn't really matter. If we believe that life begins at conception, then what difference does it make if the unborn child looks like a blood clot or a fully formed human? We cannot place more value on a child because of its stage of development in the womb or because of the circumstances under which it was conceived.

When pro-lifers buy into the lie that one child is more valuable and worthy of protection than another because it is further along or happens to be a product of a violent and inexcusable sexual act, then we are condoning the violent slaughter of children and, like the people working in POC labs across the country, we have the blood of innocents on our hands.

Abortion clinic workers have experienced evil in a very tangible way. We have seen it in the glass dishes that hold the parts of the aborted babies. We have touched evil as we reassembled those parts. And we have even smelled evil. Abortion has a very distinct smell—one that you will never be able to forget, no matter how long you have been away. That evil becomes a part of you. It's what numbs you to the brutality. It's what keeps you there every day, until the evil all around you is just all in a day's work.

14

Perks

Throughout the years I spent working in an abortion clinic, I often raved about their benefits package. I was proud to work for an organization that went out of its way to take care of their employees. And in all honesty, they really did. They offered an excellent medical and dental insurance package for employees, as well as spouses and any dependents. I had access to both short- and long-term disability insurance, ample vacation and sick time, and a 401(k) that matched up to 50 percent. Oh, and they would abort my babies free of charge. Complimentary child killing is the company car of the abortion business.

During a session at the last pro-abortion conference I attended, the speaker was discussing interpersonal relationships and how clinic staff could work together more effectively to foster an atmosphere of camaraderie. She mentioned that approximately 70 percent of Planned Parenthood employees were themselves post-abortive. We were not selling something to women that most of us hadn't also bought ourselves.

I remembered feeling good about this. As if it made our movement more authentic. We were not simply standing for a woman to have the right to choose abortion. The majority of us had also unapologetically made that choice. We knew what it was like to be in a crisis pregnancy. We could empathize.

Another perk of working at an abortion clinic was having a plethora of pregnancy tests at our disposal. I stared in disbelief at one of those tests as the plus sign slowly came into focus. Pregnant. How could this be? I faithfully popped my birth control pills to prevent this very thing. I was focused on my career, and starting a family was closer to the bottom of my to-do list. But this time was different. Although this was far from my first pregnancy, I never considered abortion as an option this time. My husband and I had been married for a few months. I knew that he would be a wonderful father, and ready or not, we were going to have a baby.

At the time, I was the lead abortion counselor at my clinic. As soon as I recovered from the shock, and the emotional dust settled, I decided to talk to my boss. *This will be weird*, I thought. A pregnant woman coaching other pregnant women about abortions.

"Do you want to just move me to the lab? Or to recovery?" I asked.

My boss barely tried to conceal her disappointment, the same disappointment that she had shown when she had found out that I was getting married. Less time and energy that I would have for my career. She had plans for me and didn't like when my life outside of the clinic got in the way.

"No," she sighed, resigned to the fact that I had resolved to carry this baby to term.

"You don't think it will make women uncomfortable? Like, as I start to show?"

"If anything, it'll encourage them to abort," she snorted. I was taken aback by her comment and quite frankly thought that she was nuts. I mean, I felt like everyone loves a hugely pregnant lady—always fawning over them and telling them that they are adorable and glowing and the like—which sounds insane since terminating pregnancies was a huge part of what we did. But in the end, she was right. I found that women either completely ignored the fact that I was hugely pregnant or went out of their way to make some sort of disparaging comment about it. I heard "Better you than me!" more times than I care to count.

I wondered if it would be weird for me to sit across the table from women and counsel them to end their pregnancies as I lovingly nurtured my own. But honestly, it wasn't. I marvel now at what a simple thinker I was—or allowed myself to be. People would ask me when I thought life began, and I would shrug and flippantly insist that I didn't know. I just did what I did.

The pro-abortion mantra, every child a wanted child, was enough for me to lay my head on the pillow at night and rest well. The children whose mothers I coaxed toward abortion were not wanted. And this time, mine was. Simple as that. I remember a conversation with one of the pro-lifers who prayed regularly outside of my clinic. He had heard that I was pregnant and wanted to congratulate me. He also gently tried to point out my baby was no different than the ones that we routinely aborted.

"Doesn't being pregnant make you question what you do?" he asked.

"Not at all," I retorted. He winced at my bluntness. "I've been pregnant three times and have made three choices. Twice to abort, and once to keep it. This child, I want."

"We are praying for you. For you and for your baby."

I thanked him. I truly was grateful, and it comforted me to know that they were praying for us. As excited as my husband and I were to become parents in a few short months, we were also petrified. And although my work friends had also congratulated us when they found out that I intended to have the baby, being a pregnant abortion clinic worker was complicated in ways I hadn't anticipated.

As is the case with most expectant mothers, my first trimester was fraught with nausea. Whoever decided to dub the malady "morning sickness" must have been a man, because my poor stomach had no sense of timing. I was sick, my friends. Sick. As much as I was determined to plow through and work through the queasiness, some days it got the better of me. I would spend my lunch breaks curled up on an exam table with a cool cloth on my face. My coworkers would pop in and out, offering ice chips and crackers. And abortion. "We can take care of that for you." "Want me to put you on the schedule?" "There is still time to change your mind, you know." "We could give you a freebie. Just one of the perks of working here!"

I reacted to their off-color comments by groaning, rolling my eyes, or playfully telling them to shut up. Jokes about terminating pregnancies are part of the abortion industry's sick little subculture. We all participated, and it seemed normal. But this was different. This was my *baby*! I wanted her. I already loved her.

Despite the secret rage and indignation that welled up in me with every mention of aborting my unborn daughter, I held my tongue and pretended to laugh along. Anyone who has known me for more than five minutes understands that not speaking my mind is entirely foreign and out of character for me. But what could I say? We routinely ended the lives of children further along than the one growing in my womb. Most of us had aborted at least once.

I began to dread going to work. I told myself that if I could just get past twenty-four weeks, they would stop. And for the most part, they did. They even threw a baby shower for me. Right there at the clinic. The irony of a baby shower at an abortion clinic didn't strike me until years later. But there was always a tension there. Behind every "congratulations" was a strange sense of unease. The precious little girl rapidly forcing my belly to expand was a constant testimony to the disturbing truth of what we did.

In his 1993 masterpiece, *Schindler's List*, director Steven Spielberg presents the World War II era's atrocities perpetrated against Jews almost exclusively in black and white. One exception, a little girl in a red coat, rivets Schindler as he watches the violent scene playing out in the Krakow ghetto. In stark contrast to the wholesale murder and unspeakable cruelties occurring all around her, the little girl in the red coat meanders through the sea of panic and desperation.

When asked about the significance of the little girl in red, Spielberg said, "America and Russia and England all knew about the Holocaust when it was happening, and yet we did nothing about it. We didn't assign any of our forces to stopping the march toward death, the inexorable march toward death. It was a large bloodstain, primary red color on everyone's radar, but no one did anything about it. And that's why I wanted to bring the color red in."[1]

---

[1] Steven Spielberg, director and producer, *Schindler's List* (Universal City, Calif.: Amblin Enterainment, 1993), film.

I believe that an obviously pregnant mother in an abortion clinic creates the same effect as that ill-fated little girl in the red coat, who is later seen by Schindler in a pile of corpses. The swollen belly of a pregnant mother is confirmation that there is life growing within her. It silently attests to the fact that the lives of countless others have been snuffed out—that their blood is on our hands.

But the blood of murdered Jews stained not only Nazis' hands, but the hands of all who knew about the slaughter and chose to look away. The violent death of millions of babies every year tarnishes not only the hands of clinic workers and consenting mothers, but the hands of all who know but refuse to speak out against the evil.

John 3:19–21 says, "And this is the judgment, that the light has come into the world, and men loved darkness rather than light, because their deeds were evil. For every one who does evil hates the light, and does not come to the light, lest his deeds should be exposed. But he who does what is true comes to the light, that it may be clearly seen that his deeds have been wrought in God."

I can't deny that the business of abortion is a lucrative one. Its laborers are well compensated with enviable benefits packages and perks. I now understand that life is God's most precious gift. It is light. And there is no darker place on earth than one that profits from the death of innocent children. Even though I was still very much a slave to my own sins and the scales were firmly affixed to my eyes, my decision to choose life for my daughter was an unwelcome touch of light in a place riddled with darkness.

15

One in 729,000

I grew up in a strong Catholic family. Abortion was never openly discussed, but I knew that it wasn't something that was condoned or acceptable in our family, end of story. When I grew up, got married, and had a large family of my own, abortion wasn't something that I thought a ton about. I believed in and supported life. My husband and I were both in college when we were married and worked different shifts. We always found a way to care for our seven children and rarely used babysitters. Unfortunately, my husband died when I was in my third year of prerequisites for the nursing program.

I only remember bits and pieces of the day that my husband died. I do distinctly remember thinking that my children had lost their father, and despite the pit that I was in emotionally, I couldn't allow them to lose me to depression. I knew that I had to rise above my own emotional turmoil and essentially be a rock star for my kids. I was thirty-two, a widow, and the sole provider for my seven beautiful children.

I struggled through a few semesters after my husband's death. The thought of providing for my children alone overwhelmed me. In the end, I graduated from the medical assistant program. I never stopped wanting to work in the health-care field. I desired this because I respected life, not because I wanted to take it.

After I graduated from the medical assistant program, the job recruiter put me in contact with a women's health clinic, and I interviewed via phone for a position with them. The man was extremely interested in me once he learned that I was Hispanic and was fluent in both English and Spanish. He hired me on the spot as a surgical assistant. I was led to believe that the organization existed to provide essential services to underprivileged women and to prevent unplanned pregnancies. Working for an abortion clinic certainly wasn't something I had ever envisioned myself doing, but I desperately needed a job, and finding work in the medical field without experience is difficult. I accepted the position.

I tried to think of the job as a fresh start for my hurting family. I wanted to keep an open mind. I was told that I would have to float throughout the clinic in order to become proficient in each area. I did lab work, ultrasounds, set up the rooms for abortions, and provided patient support. I held women's hands as their babies were aborted. I also worked in the POC (Products of Conception) lab, which saddened and sickened me so deeply that I am still haunted by the images of bloody body parts—the things I can't unsee. Yet, I stayed.

As many abortion clinics are, the one I worked at was strategically placed in a very poor and ethnically diverse section of the city. In fact, more than 70 percent of Planned Parenthood facilities are located in minority neighborhoods. The majority of our patients were Hispanic or African American, and many of them spoke very little English.

I got the feeling that these women were signing forms that they did not understand. As a Hispanic woman myself, I could speak to them. I felt that it was my responsibility to make absolutely sure that they understood their options.

One woman in particular sticks out in my mind. She had a gaggle of children. She just had one baby after another, and she was presenting for an abortion. I could tell that she felt very uneasy about this. I asked her if she wanted to see the baby or know if she was having multiples. These are questions that are supposed to be asked but unfortunately rarely are. In her case, it made a difference.

I asked her in Spanish if she wanted to see a picture and know the gestational age.

"Si," she responded.

She asked many questions about the baby and the procedure. Did the baby have a heartbeat? Would the baby feel the abortion?

"I don't think that you are sure," I told her. "This is a human being. You obviously need time to think about this."

My coworkers were less than thrilled that I was holding things up. "She's here, isn't she? She has made up her mind."

One of the doctors who spoke a smattering of Spanish heard what was going on and charged in. In a short time, he convinced her. I remember feeling so defeated—especially after she returned later to thank me for holding her hand the entire time and explaining things to her.

The longer I worked at the clinic, the more I learned that people were not doing their jobs. The person doing the ultrasounds rarely posed the questions they were supposedly required to ask. I always shared my story with patients. I was a widow and mother of seven beautiful children, and if I could do it, surely so could they.

One day, an African American woman presented to the clinic requesting an abortion. She was around twenty, very pretty, and seemed quite shy. I was struck by how tiny and delicate she looked, maybe 110 pounds soaking wet, even with her obvious baby bump. She appeared to be uncomfortable, yet resigned, to terminate the pregnancy.

After the ultrasound, other workers were called in to see the screen. I had never seen anything like it. This tiny woman was pregnant with quadruplets. They were all in the same sac, which I assumed meant that they were identical. We told her right away. Even the most seasoned worker was excited by the sight of four babies growing inside of this diminutive girl. Our ultrasound machine was so poor. The girl doing the ultrasound estimated that she was thirteen weeks pregnant, but I felt that she was much further along.

She immediately called her boyfriend. We could easily hear his response through the receiver. "It don't matter to me if there are a hundred babies," he said. "I don't want any of 'em." She tried to assert herself and make it clear that she wanted to wait a while. She needed time to think. He made it clear that if she did not abort these babies, he would not stand by her.

She began to cry. The poor thing was obviously not mentally prepared for aborting one child. The thought of four was pushing her over the edge. Upon hearing the tone of harsh indifference of the "father" over the receiver, the staff tried to persuade her to proceed with the abortion. Too distraught to make up her mind, she walked out of the clinic without a word.

Several days later, she was back with her boyfriend. She looked even tinier next to him. He was well over six feet tall, much older than her, and the first word that came to mind upon seeing him was "thug". We all felt tense around him. It was obvious that he had control over her.

"She wants an abortion. Four babies," he chuckled, shaking his head. "Anyway, I don't want any kids."

He settled into a chair in the waiting room, and we took her back for counseling. Before we could even start talking to her, she was crying again. She was not ready. She hadn't wrapped her mind around the reality of the situation. I refused to sign the paperwork. I wrote that I felt she was being coerced—not just by her boyfriend, but by our medical director who kept popping into the room and explaining how high risk a multiple pregnancy can be. She left the clinic in tears again.

Late the next afternoon we were preparing to close the clinic when she staggered in. She was clutching and cradling her stomach, moaning softly. I grabbed her by the elbow and escorted her to the back. Her boyfriend plopped into a waiting room chair and began playing on his phone.

"What did you do?" I asked, trying hard to suppress the panic I was feeling.

Apparently her boyfriend had taken her directly from our clinic to another clinic—more of a butcher shop in my opinion. They had given her a dose of misoprostol and sent her home. My face flushed with anger. I couldn't believe that someone would give a patient an abortifacient drug and let her leave. Our clinic would never have done that.

We guided her into the bathroom, undressed her from the waist down, and instructed her to sit on the toilet. We were all horrified at the events that unfolded in the next few minutes. The first baby fell into the toilet. The nurse grabbed a chux pad and held it to her bottom as we hurried her to the procedure room. It was then that the next two babies fell out and were hanging from her. The arms of the perfectly formed lifeless baby boys were wrapped around each other.

We were finally able to get her to the procedure room and started IV sedation, but she was still in so much pain. The fourth baby had had to be suctioned out of her. He came out in pieces.

I remember sobbing with a coworker as we sorted through the remains of the fourth baby boy in the POC lab. We cradled the tiny intact babies in our arms and cried for them. I knew that I could no longer do this work. I was done.

My heart broke for the young mother as she left the clinic that day. She had such an empty look in her eyes. There was no follow-up care or concern for her welfare. My coworkers and I continued to cry, which ticked off the doctor, who was extremely emotionless and matter-of-fact about things. She forbade us to discuss what had happened that day.

After the incident with the quads, I couldn't look at my own beautiful children without seeing dismembered body parts. I had nightmares in which I would be having an abortion. I could literally feel the pain in my dream. Maybe if I had explained to her how rare a spontaneous quad pregnancy was, one in 729,000 pregnancies, she would have grasped what a precious gift her babies were and these boys would have had a chance. These thoughts haunted me.

One of the pro-lifers who prayed outside of our clinic had given me a pamphlet about Abby's ministry, And Then There Were None (ATTWN). I remember taking the paper from her, not thinking much of it at the time. Today, I am so grateful that I made the call.

Abby and ATTWN helped me get my life on track. Knowing that she had also worked for Planned Parenthood and understood where I had been and what I had done made me feel less alone. She understood the pain and shame that plagued me. I am planning on attending a retreat for former workers in a few months and look forward to a new level of healing, hope, and forgiveness.

I cannot change the past, but I can speak out against the evil of abortion in my community. Through sharing what I have seen, I can help the women targeted by the abortion industry for profit choose life for their babies. I have even found love again and remarried. We are growing together in our journey with God and are even praying that we are blessed with a child of our own. Life is precious, and I am so thankful for every moment.

16

Teddy Bear

At the abortion clinic where I worked, it was our policy that women make their own appointments for their abortions. There were occasionally some exceptions, and I was on the phone with one of them.

"My daughter is sixteen. We just found out that she has been sexually abused by her stepbrother and now she is pregnant. She doesn't know what is going on. She has the mental age of a five-year-old. And I hope you don't mind, but she will bring a big teddy bear to her appointment. It's the only thing that makes her comfortable."

Her mom further explained that the stepbrother was in jail being held for the sexual assault, and that they would need us to collect the fetal tissue for the police department. That was no problem. We did that pretty frequently in cases of sexual assault.

The day of the young girl's abortion came, and I briefed the staff. I knew we had to take special care with her. I figured she would probably be confused and possibly scared.

They arrived for their appointment early. And there she was, with her teddy bear. She walked in behind her mom and stepfather. Her head was down, but she would occasionally lift her eyes to look around. Her long, blonde hair was tied back with a ribbon. She didn't look sixteen. She looked so young and innocent. Her face was beautiful and clear; it had never been touched by makeup.

I brought the family back to my office to assist them with their paperwork and to explain the details of the abortion procedure to her parents. They explained to me that they knew their daughter was twelve weeks pregnant. The mother had caught her stepson in the act. She immediately reported it to the police, who took him into custody. He had assured them that "it was the only time."

We took her back to the procedure room. I remember her on the table, her eyes darting all around the room. She was still holding on to that teddy bear. I couldn't imagine how confused she was. How would we explain the transvaginal ultrasound to her?

I walked out and found our doctor. I needed to brief him on the situation before he walked in. He was surprisingly very sympathetic. That was not his normal temperament. This particular abortionist was known for his gallows humor and crass remarks about our patients. Even after his apparent sympathy, I was still a little nervous.

Our doctor walked in, and I followed closely behind him. He walked right up to the table, looked her in the eyes, and then did something I had never seen an abortionist do before: he introduced himself. He was so soft spoken. I could barely hear what he was saying. He was explaining that he was going to be taking care of her and then started asking questions about her teddy bear, which prompted lots of conversation from her.

He continued to talk with her as he started the ultrasound. She didn't even seem to notice. But I immediately noticed something. This young girl was not twelve weeks pregnant. Her baby was sixteen weeks along.

I knew what that meant, and I honestly didn't want to deliver the news to her parents. Their little girl had been abused many times, over a longer period of time. I was devastated for them. I was devastated for this young girl.

Since our facility didn't perform abortions past fourteen weeks, I knew she would need to be referred to another provider. In my mind, I started practicing the speech I would give her parents. "Your daughter is sixteen weeks pregnant. She is too far along to have the abortion at our facility. I will provide you with a phone number to the National Abortion Federation. They will be able to help you locate a clinic that can help. You will also need to give this information to the police. You will of course want them to know that the abuse had been going on much longer than you thought." There. That sounded good. Clinical, not attached. I would just give them the information and let them process the details. After all, I was not there to be their counselor, even though the title given to me at the clinic was "abortion counselor". That was just a title. I wasn't actually anyone's counselor.

The doctor had taken several ultrasound photographs of the sixteen-week-old baby and instructed me to put one in her chart and give the others to the parents. He said they would need them to provide further evidence to the police.

As I walked out of the room with the ultrasound photos in hand, the doctor called out to me. "Get the parents in your office, and I will be in there in a second to discuss this with them," he said. *What?* I thought. *That had never happened either.*

I waited for the young girl to get dressed and escorted her to my office. I then went to the waiting room and asked her parents to come back. I could see the anxiety on their faces when they saw me come out from behind the heavy metal door.

The four of us sat in my small office. Our sweet patient was smiling at her teddy bear, occasionally making small talk with him. Her parents were across from me, staring me down with nervous faces.

Stick to the script in your head, I told myself. "Your daughter is sixteen weeks pregnant, not twelve," I began. Her mother put her hands over her mouth and began to weep. The father jumped up out of his chair, from what I assumed was either anger or shock, or maybe both. My script was falling apart. Not really knowing what else to do, I grabbed the mother's hand and encouraged the father to sit down. "We're going to help you get through this," I said.

I had already written the number to the National Abortion Federation on a business card and was just about to hand it to them when the doctor walked in. He introduced himself and sat down beside the parents. "I guess she has already given you the news?" he asked. Both of them nodded their heads in agreement. We were all silent for a minute, and then the mother finally spoke up, "What do we do now?"

The next five minutes blew my mind. The doctor proceeded to get out a pregnancy wheel and explain some dates to the parents. He was helping them understand when their daughter most likely conceived. Then he said something else that I had never heard come out of the mouth of anyone in my clinic. "I don't think it is best for your daughter to have an abortion at this point. I could certainly perform this procedure at my private clinic, but

I truly believe that an abortion is not the right answer." I couldn't believe what I was hearing. We always encouraged abortion, no matter what. What was he doing? He looked at me and said, "She will help you get the resources you guys need to parent this baby or place him or her for adoption." I probably stared at him for a good twenty seconds before responding. I quickly snapped out of it and said, "Of course!"

We didn't really have any resources in our facility on adoption or parenting, so I had to go searching on the Internet for something to print out. After about an hour of more discussion with the parents, I sent them out with a folder full of helpful information. They left with smiles on their faces, seeming very relaxed and sure of their decision *not* to abort their grandchild.

What was going on here? While I was certainly relieved that this family had made a choice that seemed right for them, I couldn't help but think that if we keep helping people choose to parent their kids, it would eventually cut into our profits. That would mean layoffs for our clinic. I figured this physician, who believed in infanticide up to twenty-four months post-birth, had just had a strange soft spot for this young girl.

A couple of weeks later, we were performing abortions again with the same doctor. A young woman came to the clinic for a first-trimester abortion. I counseled her before her abortion. She was very noticeably upset about having an abortion. I questioned her and encouraged her to maybe take some time and think about her decision. She was insistent—this abortion must happen today. This is what she wanted. She was just emotional, she said. She asked if I would be in the room with her to hold her hand during the procedure. I was happy to do that for people I counseled, especially those who were nervous or upset.

We got her in the room, and I sat down beside her. I put her blood pressure cuff on, and the sedation was given. But the sedation didn't make much difference. She cried even harder. She was shaking so hard that her body was moving off of the table. The doctor entered the room in his usual manner. He was about to sit down on his stool and realized she was very upset. Then he did something again that left me speechless.

He walked over to her and stood next to my chair. He took her hand and began talking to her. "Why the tears?" he said. "I just feel really guilty about doing this," she responded. He asked her why she felt guilty. She said, "Because I just know this is a sin." He paused for a minute and looked at her; he was looking at her so carefully, so cautiously. He smiled gently at her and said, "No. It is not your sin. It is mine. I will take on your sin. I commit the sin. Not you." He patted her hand, walked back to his stool, and sat down. Her crying immediately stopped.

Did he really think he was committing a sin? How could he do it if he really thought that? Did he think he was taking on the sins of these women by helping them obtain abortions? What a heavy burden to bear. It was hard for me to process.

If he really believed what he said, he was intentionally taking on the sins of these women. Why would he do that? Why would he want to? I won't ever know the answer to these questions, but I do know that sin doesn't work that way. He can't be the scapegoat for these women.

I think both of these scenarios give us a glimpse into the heart of an abortionist. Have they become blinded by their sin? Yes. Are they redeemable? Absolutely. We desperately try to blame someone for the number of abortions that take place in our world. And many times that blame falls to the physicians performing them. But is that blame misplaced? I believe it is. Our enemy is not those inside the abortion facilities. Our enemy is not the woman who seeks abortion services. Our true enemy is sin. As a former abortion clinic worker, my goal is to tell everyone that conversion can happen to anyone. We shouldn't ever limit God by our own earthly expectations.

17

Want It More

I was very young when I first heard about monks who burned themselves in protest. Of course, that wasn't the kind of thing taught in my first grade class, but I heard it referenced on the news or caught bits and pieces of information in adult conversations. The thought of it captivated me in a morbid way, like a young moth drawn to a desperate and dramatic flame half a world away.

Since I had experienced the intense pain of a mere splash of boiling oil on my skin, the thought of a sane human being drenched in gas and set ablaze, all the while maintaining the lotus position, blew my little mind. My morose fascination with the phenomenon never left me, and when I was older I read everything I could on the subject.

"Self-immolation" is the term most commonly used for the act of committing suicide as a form of protest or self-sacrifice, typically referring to setting oneself on fire. The West became aware of this practice in June of 1963 when a Vietnamese Buddhist monk named Thích Quảng Đức assumed the lotus position at a busy intersection in Saigon. After a fellow monk doused him with gasoline, Đức struck a match and dropped it on himself.

This act of protest against the persecution of Buddhists by the South Vietnamese government was captured by

American journalist and photographer Malcom Browne. Browne's graphic photograph of the self-immolation spread like wildfire of its own, and soon it was featured on the front page of newspapers around the globe. Of the photo, then-President Kennedy said, "No news picture in history has generated so much emotion around the world as that one."[1]

It was this intense emotion that piqued my interest, even as a little girl. The idea that he could be so deeply committed to his cause that he would be able to sit serenely as his flesh was literally burning was beyond my comprehension. But in a way, I admired it. Unlike suicide bombers who sacrifice themselves with the hope of taking as many innocent bystanders as possible with them, these monks were willing to die a horrific death in order to draw attention to their cause and benefit others.

Please don't think that I am advocating that folks set themselves ablaze to protest abortion. The taking of life has never, and will never, advance the pro-life cause. Quite the opposite is true. In a way, I think this twisted admiration and idealization of those willing to sacrifice themselves for what they believed in drew me into a career in the abortion industry. Even in the early stages of my involvement in the abortion faction, I became aware that abortion advocates were rabidly committed to their cause. They were willing to surrender anything, including their lives, to ensure that women continued to have access to abortion on demand.

As clinic director, random attacks or bombings were constantly in the forefront of my mind. FBI agents and

[1] Seth Jacobs, *Cold War Mandarin: Ngo Dinh Diem and the Origins of America's War in Vietnam, 1950–1963* (Lanham, Md.: Rowman & Littlefield, 2006), p. 149.

marshals provided regular trainings for workers. They taught us the basics of doing a bomb sweep and gave step-by-step instructions for what to do once a bomb threat was received. They also gave suggestions for how to protect ourselves outside of the clinic: Don't travel the same route to and from work. Keep your address and phone numbers unlisted. Don't give your personal information to anyone.

The National Abortion Federation also sent directors a weekly email called "Hotspots" that provided a list of potential threats and protester activity. Some of these threats were completely legitimate. Others were trumped-up and involved something as harmless as a phone call or letter simply stating that someone was praying for them. For the abortion industry, any hindrance to providing abortions is treated as a threat.

The threats, both real and imagined, only strengthened our resolve and commitment to the cause. A well-known abortionist slain by a pro-lifer while serving at his church was practically a saint to us. He was our example to follow. He didn't let the anti-choice terrorists win, even though it cost him his life. Even after six very specific threats on my life, I was undeterred. Not because I wasn't scared. I was terrified. Some of these threats came to my home and mentioned my husband and child by name. My daughter would be much better off having no mother than a mother like me, one of them said.

As the threats continued, my family began to take them more seriously. My clinic installed a security system outside of our house. By the fifth threat, it hit me that I was more angry than scared. I was like, "Okay then! Go ahead! Where are you?" It started to feel like a joke to me. Whatever the intention of the creeper, who for whatever sick reason felt the need continually to threaten my life, I am pretty sure it had the opposite effect. I felt even more invested in what I was doing.

If there was one thing that I could make the pro-life camp understand about the people who are entrenched in the abortion movement, it would be this: we saw abortion as a civil rights issue. In our minds, we were fighting against a movement that wanted to rip away the rights of women—a battle similar to the ones fought to give women the right to vote or to end segregation. We were willing to sacrifice to an extent that I have unfortunately not seen in the pro-life movement.

Our physical safety wasn't the only thing that was on the line. Another tactic employed by a fringe element of the pro-life movement was to call out abortion workers in their communities in an attempt to shame them. One protester went so far as to look up my license plate number and send postcards to our entire neighborhood "outing" me as an abortion worker. He equated me with a child molester. Again, this method backfired when students and single mothers in the poor area where we lived came to me asking for free birth control. Even though my parents were not supportive of my involvement in the industry, after the death threats and mailings, they were much more sympathetic toward me and began to regard pro-life activists as dangerous, crazy people.

In addition, the rhetoric of the other side only enforced the divide and solidified in our minds that we were soldiers in a feminist holy war of sorts. Now that the spiritual blindfold has been removed and I understand the evil I was participating in, I get it. I do. But I must appeal to pro-lifers to please consider the language they use when they have occasion to converse with clinic workers and women in crisis pregnancies. Use that opportunity to show them how much you have in common. Kindness, grace, and love bathed in prayer can pierce even the hardest heart. Harsh verbiage, like the other failed strategies, achieves nothing and only drives the wedge deeper. If your goal is to cultivate a culture of life, please delete the following terms from your vocabulary when communicating with the other side: deathscort, abortuary, slaughterhouse, death mill, death chamber, planned barrenhood, klan parenthood. You get the picture.

The fringe element of the pro-life movement who prefers to employ tactics that heavily rely on shock value fails to understand one thing: the more extreme their behavior, the more hardened we became. Both the clinic workers and the women in crisis pregnancies regarded them as crazy freaks. We need to think, people! In what world would a woman run to a person dressed like the Grim Reaper marching on the sidewalk outside an abortion clinic to ask for help with her crisis pregnancy? Will a teen, already terrified of being judged by her religious parents, run to protesters outside the clinic hurling Bible verses at her like bullets, never offering a solution or help? No. All too often, the insane, self-righteous behavior drove them into our waiting arms. It built camaraderie inside the clinic and made our job, which was ultimately to sell abortion, exceedingly easier.

Here is the bottom line. These clinic workers—from the owner, to the abortionist, to the nurses and receptionists—have bought in to the spiritual deception that abortion is the right thing to do. They are, like I once was, fully convinced of this deep in their hearts. And they are willing to risk their lives and their reputations for what they consider to be the civil right of abortion on demand. Sadly enough, they want it more. They are willing to risk more.

This inequity is most glaringly obvious when it comes to fundraising. The fundraisers of abortion rights groups were always well attended. Several thousand politicians, actors, actresses, and other influential people would pack in. There were usually a large number of clergy who would attend our events, and we would always recognize them. Their presence helped normalize abortion and made us feel even better about our mission. Without even having to make a big appeal, we would rake in several million dollars in a single evening. When an abortion affiliate decided to build a new facility to the tune of seventeen million dollars, the money was raised quickly with little effort.

I have heard a lot of pro-lifers chime in on this phenomenon. Some say that is because abortion advocates don't have children. That simply isn't true. They have families just like we do. Some say they have more expendable income. While this may be true in some cases, I do not believe that this is the heart of the issue either. The fact is that the people who are committed to the abortion movement are willing to sacrifice their time, talents, and treasure in a way that I have not seen elsewhere.

Speaking of this gap in enthusiasm and commitment between the pro-life and pro-abortion movements, Pennsylvania politician Rick Santorum said, "They're passionate; they're willing to do and say uncomfortable things in mixed company. They're willing to make the sacrifice at their business because they care enough."[2]

---

[2] Rick Santorum, "Liberals 'Make It Uncomfortable for Students' to Shower at the Gym", *Huffington Post*, August 7, 2013, http://www.huffingtonpost.com /2013/08/07/rick-santorum-showers_n_3718618.html.

I am afraid that he's right. But I am also encouraged by some subtle shifts I am seeing in the movement to end abortion. It seems to me that there are two types of pro-lifers active in the cause. The first simply wants to win, and in their minds, they do this by saving the baby. They are right fighters who don't seem to give any consideration to the other lives involved, such as the mother, father, and clinic workers. Their goal is to save the *baby* at all costs.

Of course we all want to save the baby, but the second group of people I see in the movement have realized that the hearts, minds, and souls of many others are at stake as well. These are the people who excite me and encourage me on a daily basis. They are the people who want to help in any way possible. They want to provide so many avenues of support that abortion would be unthinkable. They offer solutions instead of slogans, prayers instead of protests, self-sacrifice instead of self-righteousness.

It is this peaceful, prayerful approach that we all need to adopt. Yes, we need highly trained sidewalk counselors to connect with women and help them find a solution for their unique situations. Remember, inside the clinic, we don't offer options or solutions. We only offer abortion. If we want to save the baby, we must connect with and provide practical help to the woman so that she won't consider abortion as her only option.

If you aren't properly trained to talk to women in crisis, please know that you still need to show up. I cannot stress that enough. Show up. When it is hot and humid, show up. When it is freezing, show up. The prayers of the people outside were a big factor in my ultimately leaving the abortion industry.

If the prayer volunteers hadn't shown up each and every day, I wonder if I would have been able to suppress or somehow justify the truth of what I was doing when it was finally revealed to me. Without their presence, could I have pushed that knowledge away and continued on with what seemed like the easier option? Without their prayers, would I have stayed at my high-paying job where I was on track to be the next chief operating officer? Without people standing outside the fence praying, just praying, I don't know if I could have left.

Our movement has a long way to go. I know I have outlined a lot of the negatives, but we need to acknowledge our mistakes and stop the ineffectual and insane tactics that have stereotyped all pro-lifers and caused abortion-minded women to run into the clinics for several decades. Out with the old, and in with the new.

I tell people all the time, you have to go. You must be present outside of the clinics because you don't have any idea what might be going on inside. Some people are worried about being labeled a zealot or a freak. It doesn't matter what people think of you. Some people are concerned about saying the wrong thing. If you aren't trained, don't say anything. Just be there and pray.

Your presence will matter. A seed of doubt will be planted in the minds of women entering the clinic. I've never seen a protester holding a sign or praying outside of my dentist's office. Why? Because there is nothing morally objectionable about filling a cavity. The physical presence outside of the clinic reminds people that there is something very wrong happening in those buildings. You need not wear lab coats stained with fake blood or dangle plastic doll parts from your cars to illustrate the point. Your commitment to being there despite the inconvenience and discomfort says it all.

The abortion industry is a well-funded giant with immense community support. Still, they fear us. Why? The last conference I attended had a workshop about how to handle protesters. The speaker said that when people show up outside the clinic, the no-show rate goes up to almost 75 percent. Three-quarters of abortion-minded women will simply not show up if there is a presence on the sidewalk.

We don't have to burn ourselves in protest as Thích Quảng Đức did in 1963. The answer is so simple. You want to help end abortion? Just show up. Find a peaceful, prayerful group of people in your area who are committed to life, and join them. This is how God will use us to end the evil of abortion. Put yourself out there and trust him to do the rest.

FINAL THOUGHTS FROM ABBY

You have made it through this book. I wonder what you are feeling right now. Anger? Sadness? Maybe a little bit of both. Let's take some time and address those feelings.

I am vehemently against the death penalty. Now stay with me—this chapter is not about my opinion regarding that. You can disagree or agree with me on that some other time. I did want to share a little bit about why I take the words of pro-lifers so seriously. I have heard so much vitriol spewed from the mouths of "Christian pro-lifers" since becoming pro-life. I feel that we must address these sorts of issues so we can make our movement as strong as it can be.

When I was confirmed as a Catholic, I chose Mary Magdalene as my confirmation saint. I felt an immediate connection to her. She had sinned so much—and was forgiven in even greater amounts. She knew she didn't deserve forgiveness—but she received it anyway. And because of this, she clung to Christ. She knew she was nothing without him.

I have also done my fair share of sinning. And I have also been forgiven much more than I deserve. I abused and betrayed women in the worst possible way. I convinced them to kill their children. Did I hold the suction probe that actually ended their lives? No. But I was an accomplice to murder—thousands of times, involving women

I knew, women I didn't, my friends, even my family. I lied to people. I lied to women when they came to me for accurate information. I was among the worst sinners—those that help to take and destroy life.

I took my own children's lives—twice. Not because I was coerced; not because I didn't know better. But because I thought children would be an inconvenience to my lifestyle. I am responsible for their deaths—no one else.

So when someone talks about abortion clinic workers or abortionists and says things like, "Murderers and people like them don't deserve to breathe the same air as I do," or "I hope they burn in hell," it hurts a little, because that was me. But I am still here, breathing that same air and trying to spend my life righting my wrongs. And it's not just me. I know these words hurt others like me as well—people who have left the abortion industry and will work every day to recover from their sins. People who are still in the industry and think they will be shunned by the pro-life movement—maybe they would reach out to us if they knew we would accept them. I am always terrified that clinic workers will see some of the words from pro-lifers. I have been told by several former workers that they will *never* come forward with their stories, because they are so scared of how they will be treated by us—by *us*, the supposed "Christian" movement. Their fears are real *and* legitimate.

I know some will say, "But you repented; that is the difference." But what if I hadn't—not yet. What if I were still inside the abortion industry? What if I were still an accomplice to murder? What if it took me longer to realize the truth? Do I deserve to die? Are we saying repentance is about our timing? Certainly, it is not about us. It is about God and his perfect timing.

Right now, I shouldn't be in this movement. I should be the chief operating officer of the fourth largest revenue-generating Planned Parenthood affiliate in the country. I should be overseeing the largest abortion facility in the Western Hemisphere. I should be making six times the amount of money that I make in the pro-life movement. But I'm not. Why? Because of forgiveness. Because of mercy. Because of grace. Because of God. And because of *real* pro-lifers. The people I turned to accepted me for me—baggage and all. They knew that I was a broken person, and they loved me anyway. They knew I needed significant healing, and they helped to provide it.

I remember one story in particular that always makes me tear up when I think about it. One of the ladies that immediately befriended me after I left Planned Parenthood (Karen) was asked a question by a reporter. He asked her, "So, what was Abby like before she became pro-life? I mean, how nasty was she?" Karen's answer was so genuine, and so Christlike. She simply said, "I don't remember that person. She is a new creation in Christ. I won't talk about her past; I only want to talk about her future." Wow. What grace. What forgiveness. She could have really spilled the beans on me, but she chose not to. Why? Because she truly loved me—and she always had, even while I was working at Planned Parenthood. She always believed the best in me, always believed that my conversion would happen.

It was Christ who changed me. It was the merciful and compassionate words of his people. It was no condemnation. It was not prayers that I would burn in hell. It was not those who yelled and called me names. It was the words of people like Karen—those who prayed that

I would, one day, walk out of that clinic; those who had constant faith, even when that faith was a struggle to have. I am here because of *them* and because of their Christ-like witness.

Don't we want that for every abortion clinic worker and abortion provider? I smile every time I imagine an abortionist converting on the issue of life. What a heavenly victory it must be! Does it happen? If you say no, then you do not know the God that I do. My God is in the business of miracles. And my God does not want anyone to suffer in hell. He wants *all* of his children to come to him—yes, even those of us "monsters" that are in or have been in the abortion industry.

Hate comes from hell. Mercy comes from Christ. When we have hate in our hearts, our spirits are damaged. Be careful with your words. Not only are you a living witness of Christ and his truth, but you could put your own soul at risk. "Any one who hates his brother is a murderer, and you know that no murderer has eternal life abiding in him" (1 John 3:15). When we hate, we are no better than those who kill.

I am not the sweetest person. I'm not the one who catches all the flies with honey; sometimes I am all vinegar. What do you expect? You expect the most tenderhearted to work in the abortion industry? Maybe we aren't like all of you. Maybe we aren't the most kindhearted. Maybe you don't understand how we could do what we have done. But those of us that leave, we are fighters. We are willing to take hits for our former sins. We are willing to stand up in places that are uncomfortable. We are willing to be bruised by others because we know that we have to; we know that will be the price we pay. It just hurts more when the bruises come from those who should be rejoicing in our repentance. We are passionate. We don't waste time beating around the bush—not when it comes to life, especially the lives that we helped take.

Those of us that have worked in the industry all live our lives with a constant burden, one that will not be free from us until we reach heaven. We can't let our burden slide off of our shoulders; it is what keeps us on fire. It reminds us of why we fight so hard. We have seen death and evil in a way that most haven't—and we participated. We are forgiven.

So, should I be able to "breathe the same air as you"? That's not really up to me to decide. But if you say things like that, know that a small piece of each of our hearts is broken, and I have to believe that it grieves Christ. But even if you break our hearts, we forgive you. Even if you bruise us, we forgive you. He who has been forgiven much, loves much. And we love a lot. I am eagerly awaiting the day when we can call all abortionists and clinic workers former and *repentant* abortion providers.

Pray for those who have contributed to this book. Pray for their continued healing. And most of all, pray for those who have not converted yet. We are waiting for them with our arms wide open.

Abby Johnson and her ministry,
"And Then There Were None" (ATTWN)

encourages and helps those who are
presently working in the abortion industry
to find new employment and joy for life
outside the abortion clinic walls.

To find out more about Abby Johnson
and her ministry, visit
And Then There Were None
www.AbortionWorker.com